Do Not Think It Strange

Jennifer Muthoni

www.apostolos-publishing.com

FAITHBUILDERS

Do Not Think It Strange by Jennifer Muthoni

First Published in Great Britain in 2019

Apostolos Publishing Ltd,
3rd Floor, 207 Regent Street,
London W1B 3HH

www.apostolos-publishing.com

A catalog record for this book is available from the British Library

ISBN: 978-1-912120-09-3

Cover Design by Apostolos Publishing Ltd. Cover Image © Rafael Ben Ari | Dreamstime.com

Printed and bound in Great Britain by Marston Book Services Limited, Oxfordshire.

CONTENTS

ACKNOWLEDGEMENTS

My heartfelt thanks to all who have encouraged and prayed with me during very difficult situations. Many thanks to Jan of HCC, who has been such an inspiration, for her significant input. Thanks also to Ken of Light House and Heidi formerly of HCC, whose computer skills were of great help to me. Finally, my thanks go to Laura and Mathew and all at Apostolos who have helped me bring this book to completion.

INTRODUCTION

We all go through difficult times. Whether we refer to these times as tough times, trials, adversity or troubles, they are all an expression of the same meaning. The Bible uses these phrases too. Perhaps the most appropriate word to describe all these experiences is "affliction."

Even the mention of phrases such as these can trigger painful memories of the troubles many of us have been through. We all want to forget the hard times, especially when they caused untold suffering and distress, leaving us traumatised with permanent scars. On a positive note, remembering may be the first thing we need to do, as it is the way that healing begins.

Troubles come to us in all different shapes and sizes. Some are huge and others small, some mild, some weighty. However, in whatever shape and form they come, they cause pain, despair and feelings of hopelessness. The consequences can be visible to others but often the scars are internal, seen and felt only by ourselves. In our state of perplexity, we are left with many unanswered questions for which only God has the answers.

Although troubles are common to all, we all respond to them differently. For some, suffering produces a reliance on God, while others are pushed farther from Him. For those who hold on, God always brings a good outcome. When we are hard pressed and in despair, our comfort and hope come as we are reminded of how Jesus bore our sorrows. Therefore, during such times we must look up to the cross, the place where every adversity was turned into good. The work that Jesus accomplished was inclusive of the troubles that have come our way.

Yet we still wonder sometimes, during such circumstances, why we experience such pain and distress if Jesus has already taken our pains and sorrows. These questions are legitimate, but only a glimpse of heaven is enough to satisfy our quest for answers. Whether it makes sense or not there are two things we can do during troubles. One is to appreciate and give thanks and be grateful for what Christ has done on the cross. Another is to remember that there is an eternity where trouble will never enter. We may not fully understand, but as our hearts overflow with thankfulness, the peace that follows is an assurance of a hope which is not in vain. Sometimes we are changed through troubles so that we may become more like Jesus, in bearing His character. These changes that occur in our character will be discussed in more detail in a later chapter.

After Job went through many troubles, we see an astounding remark that he made which shows that he gained good from his troubles. Although he had suffered so much, the returns were priceless and precious. "Seeing God," he said (Job 42:5). It is my hope we too can also say we have seen Him, for when we see Him, we shall see that all our troubles have been placed upon Him. As we behold Him our faces become radiant instead of displaying sorrow, despair and hopelessness.

Troubles are numerous and common, but not strange. This book deals with the common troubles we encounter in our lives, how to respond to them and how our hope remains, no matter what life throws at us—this is the secret of holding on.

Every chapter ends with a prayer, for we all know that the mountains and storms of life are moved by prayers of faith in God who is greater than our troubles. During difficult times prayer overrides any suggestions or good advice we may receive from others. If you, like Job, have already had everything restored after afflictions, and may not feel there is anything in this book for you, do join with me as we pray for those still in the stage of waiting—that they will still hold on to hope.

CHAPTER 1: COMMON DYNAMICS

We always hope for the best. We anticipate what is good for us and for those we love. It is no surprise then, that when adversity comes upon us our human instinct is to wonder what this strange happening is about. Having gone through tough times most of my life, I must admit there were moments when I questioned "why," and "why me?" Other times were thoughts of what was this strange thing happening to me? What might come next and what was going to be the outcome of it all?

We soon get lost in our wrestling when trouble comes, like someone in a maze who goes back and forth trying to find their way out. Job was caught unawares by the troubles that came upon him suddenly. The sequence of how it all happened would have made anyone think it strange, and so do we when we are surrounded and overwhelmed, we find ourselves questioning God and having many doubts. Trouble is a common phenomenon to all humankind.

Troubles come into our lives like intruders. They disrupt our plans, goals and seem to overthrow the purpose God has for each one of us. To make matters worse they do not just come and go, but often they linger, causing a lot of pain and suffering. However, one thing is certain. If we belong to God we are changed for the better. Jesus had to bear the same afflictions, hence His assuring exhortation "Take heart; in this world you will have trouble" (John 16:33). The psalmist also expressed how troubles come upon us in great numbers and even though they do, our good Lord always brings a good outcome.

> Many are the afflictions of the righteous, but the Lord delivers him out of them all. (Psalm 34:19)

In order to shift from a position of asking "why me?" or thinking of our troubles as strange, I feel that exploring other aspects that we have in common is important. Hopefully next time we are in trouble we will not think it strange or ask, "why me?" Our goal instead, would be taking a position of anticipating a good outcome despite the suffering trouble brings.

For many of us, our suffering leads us to a place of exploration, where we can take stock. As I searched the scriptures to discover the common dynamics of human affliction, I gained wonderful insights about adversity. Through that journey it occurred to me that in order for our questions to cease we must first find a place to start. That place is God's word. The Bible says:

> But the path of the righteous is like the light of dawn, which shines brighter and brighter until full day. (Proverbs 4:18)

As we wrestle with our difficult circumstances and look to God and His word there is a gleam of light amid our affliction. There are certain things which the Bible says we all have in common, whether we claim to know God or not. The Bible clearly teaches that:

We Are Created in God's Image

Every human being is created in the likeness of God. This is confirmed to us by the scriptures and through our relationship with the Holy Spirit who reveals all things to us.

> So God created man in his own image, in the image of God he created him; male and female he created them. (Genesis 1:27)

We all hold a certain concept of what the image of God looks like. We have also come across many ideas of what God looks like, through pictures drawn by artists, or from books we have read and movies we have seen. Yet this image is only what we see with our natural eyes.

Our conclusions about that image are based on our human perception. While it is beyond our comprehension to understand the nature of God, we are nevertheless God's image bearers. From the scriptures we can learn and understand that the image of God is more than appearance. The Bible tells us how God fashioned the man from the dust of the earth, like an artist using sand. After He had formed him, He then breathed His life into him and due to the breath of God, he became a living being with the image of God engraved in him. Every human being is a bearer of God's life which is embedded in our total being.

Therefore, whenever we look at one another we look beyond what we can see with our natural eyes and we see the image of God within every person. To understand this more, let us remember what

Samuel did when God asked him to anoint one of the sons of Jesse to be King, we read in the following account:

> Samuel saw Eliab and thought "surely the Lord's anointed stands here before the Lord" But the Lord said to Samuel, "Do not consider his appearance or his height, for I have rejected him. The Lord does not look at things man looks at. Man looks at the outward appearance, but the Lord looks at the heart." (1 Samuel 16:6–7)

This oversight of Samuel's is something we are all sometimes guilty of. We look and making judgements according to what we see, but the Lord knows how we are made. Therefore, the Lord always corrects us gently and through love and patience we learn and grow. God did not interrupt Samuel as he presented to Him all the sons of Jesse one by one but was patiently waiting.

This scripture is an invitation for us to change our concept of the image of God from one which is based on outward appearance. Jesus told the disciples seeing Him was seeing the Father (John 14:9), an image that is seen in a physical sense. Samuel's judgment was misleading because it came from the natural realm. The vision seen by the heart is superior, supernatural and real, but it can only be perceived through faith.

Therefore, if we want to understand this image more clearly, we must step away from human logic and our own perception. As God's children we no longer reason according to human logic but by the revelation of the Holy Spirit. The Bible clearly says we were created in God's image and God is the Father of all mankind. If we are not yet fully like Him in every aspect, this is because of the effects of the fallen creation upon our natures.

For all those who are called by the name of the Lord and have now been adopted as His, the effects of the fallen nature are progressively wearing away. As we become more and more like Jesus, His image will reflect in us day by day, through and through, inside and out. By the time we reach our destination we will be fully like Him. Our distorted image will one day be fully restored to its original state: perfect, beautiful and permanent.

We Live on a Common Planet

> The God, who made the world and everything in it, is the Lord of heaven and earth. From one man, He made every nation of men that they should inhabit the whole earth. (Acts 17:24–26)

This scripture helps us to understand that this planet is our common habitat, another common dynamic in human life. Planet Earth was created for us by God as a habitable place, with a viable environment for our survival. Before we came here it was in existence and we found a ready-made planet with all the goodness, resources and the very fresh air we inhale daily. It was also meant to hold us and cannot crumble under our weight, neither can it be removed. No wonder the psalmist acknowledged that the earth is firmly established, it cannot be moved.

> He set the earth on its foundations, it can never be moved. (Psalm 104:5)

In God we are secure, for it is His intention to keep the earth firmly sustained. In essence, this earth is ours and is our common habitation. If we could only grasp that the world was freely given to us by God, we would care for it. Everything that God created in the whole of the universe displays beauty. Though it is not in its original beauty, it still looks beautiful and it gives us great joy. As children of God we too should tend it and maintain it in the same state of beauty.

There is a Common Good

We were all created to do good, and there are a lot of good things we can do from the moment we rise in the morning. These good things are waiting to be done no matter where we happen to be at any given moment. The list is endless, and there is enough work for all of us to do. God is the author of work, and He is never short of ideas. Everyday has something for us to do, which God prepared before we came into being.

> For we are God's workmanship created in Christ Jesus to do good works which God prepared in advance for us to do. (Ephesians-2:10)

We are called to work and do good as unto the Lord with joy using the strength and wisdom which He has given us. In case you might be asking yourself what is that common good? Here is a summary:

a) To love and worship God and bring glory to Him.
b) To love and care for one another.
c) To take care of the environment and everything in it.

This is our job description for which I believe we are accountable to Jesus Himself. In simple terms it is His company and we have been offered the job, hence we accept and do it not out of compulsion but willingly because we are His children. As we follow His example, with His power and the strength He gives, we will find fulfilment no matter how menial the task may be. Throughout the Gospels we see the many roles Jesus played. He was a carpenter, teacher, and healer. In fact, the list is endless. Without diminishing or considering any job less noble, Jesus willingly took the role of a servant.

Every place He went, as recorded in all the four Gospels, He did good. When we do good, whether towards God, people or creation, God is glorified, and it pleases Him as He sees us becoming like Jesus in every aspect of our lives.

Life throws us a lot of troubles that we do not expect. Even when, for whatever reason, we find ourselves lonely, we can still accomplish the common good. God makes this possible for He is our helper, the One who is everywhere. We are never alone and as we worship Him, it is also counted as good. Trouble or no trouble, our common good is engraved in our being and that is the reason why we can dispense it anytime, anywhere, and to anyone.

Common Prayer

And when you pray do not keep on babbling like pagans, for they think they will be heard because of their many words. (Matthew 6:7)

I mentioned earlier that not everyone believes we were all created by God and there is a parallel to this where prayer is concerned. Most people pray, though perhaps to many gods not necessarily to God the creator. When God created us and placed eternity in every person's heart, it was to sensitise us that we might seek and know Him. That connection with Him comes through prayer and that is why prayer is of utmost importance to a Christian. We are not in the same position as non-Christians, whose prayers to their gods do not get any answers (Isaiah 46:7). Our God is living, and He has promised to hear and answer our prayers.

Prayer is something we can all have in common, most of the time about the difficult circumstances in our lives. When we are in despair due to the situations of life, we may resort to prayer. Even some who claim to be atheists have come to a time in their lives when they have prayed. I remember during my working career as a nurse, whenever someone asked me (without compunction) to pray with them, I gladly led them to the Lord in prayer. In the above scripture Jesus was addressing people who believed in God yet prayed amiss.

Paul had a similar observation when he visited Athens. He noted that the people of that town were very religious. They worshiped many idols and even a god whom they did not know (Acts 17:23). This shows how common prayer is to humanity.

Some pray during special occasions such as celebrations of events—for example, weddings, funerals and during religious practises. All who are called by the Name of the Lord pray not only when troubles come, and not only when there are special occasions, but all the time. Prayer is meant to be a lifestyle that honours and reverences our Father in heaven, the only true God. In a later chapter we will discuss prayer in more depth.

A Common Enemy

If you are a Christian the devil became your enemy the day Jesus translated you from the kingdom of darkness into His kingdom of light. When we renounced Satan as our master and accepted Jesus, the One who created and died for us, we became the devil's opponent. We have renounced the devil and his control over us. He has no more claim over us. We moved out of his camp, our rightful owner is Jesus Christ and we belong to Him forever. Sadly, for those who have not yet renounced their worldly master (the devil) he is still an enemy but presents himself as an angel of light so that he can conceal his real identity.

For Satan himself masquerades as an angel of light. (2 Cor 11:14)

Satan's only aim is to destroy. Often, he uses people to do his work through deception. The Bible warns us about his wicked plans. He is a liar who does not want to go to his final punishment with his angels alone. He wants to take as many people with him as he can. He uses his crafty and cunning ways to make it look as if he is our friend. Just as he deceived our first parents (Adam and Eve) into believing he was a good friend, giving good advice. He is a common enemy to all humanity but he has never learned any new tricks, therefore we can know his schemes.

Just to mention here in relation to troubles that for those who are in Christ, we will experience more troubles when we renounce the devil, since we are now on the offensive! The good news is, however, that we walk and live from the point of victory through Jesus our Master.

Common Afflictions

When God told Adam and Eve, after they had sinned, that the ground would produce thorns and thistles, they might have not fully understood the implication of it all at that moment. But later, it all became clear, especially when Cain murdered his brother Abel (Genesis 4:8).

Thorns and thistles represent every adversity which became the order of this world the aftermath of the fall. Although at this time we still suffer, Jesus came to restore the original plan of creation. While we groan together with all creation in our pain, we look to that day of restoration with eyes of faith, not measuring events by what we see, feel or experience during tough times.

I sat with a group of Christians gathered in a prayer meeting. Before we bowed down to pray, the leader of the group asked if there was anyone who had a prayer need. As each person shared their request, I felt inclined to write each one of them down and was struck by the fact that no prayer request was similar to the other. One thing I did notice however—they were troubles that I and many other people have experienced. To me all these prayer requests seemed overwhelming and I felt discouraged. Then immediately I had another feeling of hope because God is never overwhelmed by the number of prayer requests that bombard heaven every moment. He opens His arms and satisfies every living thing and that is our assurance as we pray. I too was ready to engage with God in praying for those who had shared their requests and for my own too.

Troubles bring a lot of pain that affects every part of who we are. However, through His Holy Spirit and His word, we have God's assurance that His promises never fail. This truth is what we stand on, during prayer. We are encouraged and wait in hope for the answer to our prayers. As I left the meeting that day, my understanding of how we share common trials was another step out of the maze into the sunshine.

Prayer

Our Father in heaven, thank You that You have adopted us into Your family through the price paid by Jesus our Saviour. Holy Spirit stamp these truths in our hearts so that we may better understand our afflictions in the light of Your word and that we may live in hope as we await Your deliverance. Amen.

CHAPTER 2: THOUGHTS & IMAGINATIONS

Do not conform any longer to the pattern of this world, but be
transformed by the renewing of your mind. (Romans 12:2)

When God created us, He endowed us with imaginations. There is
nothing wrong with imagination, but when our imaginations wander
from the will of God, then we need to take care to bring down such
imaginations. For all those in Christ the solution is found in the above
scripture. Our mind must be renewed by the word of God, which leads
to transformation. As we allow the word and the Holy Spirit to renew
our minds then every imagination will be aligned with God's will.
When calamities occur, and in times of intense suffering, many people
easily fall to the temptation of thinking that they are being punished by
God.

As we explore how our minds are affected by our afflictions, my
prayer and hope is that, by the time we come to the end of this chapter,
the Holy Spirit will give us a fresh insight and a clearer view of the
purpose of our troubles. Remember that God is love and His plans for
all people are good. As such we should never be tempted when we are
in trouble to think or say, "God is punishing us." Our inclination as
human beings during tough times or when things go wrong is to look
for an explanation for why we are afflicted. As we search for answers,
and due to the hopelessness of the situation, it is easy to blame God, the
devil, other people, or even ourselves.

Blame is a trait of the old nature and we can trace it back to the
garden of Eden. But Jesus has set us free from blaming. During many
times of severe hardship when everything seems very dark and gloomy,
I easily forget that blame was nailed to the cross. There was such a time
I vividly remember, being pushed to the edge by pain and despair until
my mind became irrational. I was in a dark pit following my divorce.
Feeling forsaken, abandoned, rejected and alone, I could not turn to
God, for I knew He hates divorce. Therefore I reasoned that He was not
going to be concerned with the state I was in. I was so alone, even my
Christian friends or family were nowhere to be found.

Later I realised that God had been there all the time in the pit
with me, but I did not know this at the time. An overwhelming surge of

love alerted me of His presence. He assured me that I had not committed any unpardonable sin. He also reminded me that as far as the east is to the west that is how far He had cast away my sins. What else could anyone need? Christ is enough in any situation. A new mindset is crucial if we are to become the people God wants us to be. Those of us who are growing and living in His grace and love are not alone in our struggles. Jesus had to bear and taste our human frailties, therefore He understands and knows our struggles.

During the hardest times, if our focus is on our circumstances, then we will be consumed by our own imaginations and faulty reasonings. No doubt the troubles may be real but our thinking about them may be completely of the old nature, instead of the new. As God's children we cannot live with the same mindset if we are to be in line with His will. There is an incidence in the Bible where the disciples of Jesus reasoned according to their own thinking and they asked Jesus:

> His disciples asked him, "Rabbi, who sinned, this man or his parents
> that he was born blind"? (John 9:2).

They looked at the condition of the man in front of them—who had been born blind-- and from it, they reasoned in their minds, wrongly, that the condition had been caused by sin. Whenever we start questioning and analysing, the mind tries to find reasons behind our problems. We have a choice to either use our imaginations for evil or good. The disciples had come to the wrong conclusion, but Jesus is always handy with the right answers. When we are faced with difficult situations instead of reasoning, blaming, or trying to figure things out, He is the answer.

Whenever we are hard pressed, our human nature tends to look for some mechanism of coping with the trouble and that mechanism can take us on the wrong path of blaming. In our vulnerability and hardship anything that will bring comfort to our troubled mind is easily welcomed. Let me share with you four aspects of misconceived thought that is important for us as Christians to be aware of, for the sake of the harvest. As we share the gospel with others, our thoughts and actions towards the lost is more important. It is said that "people don't care how much we *know* as Christians until they know how much we *care*."

Is God Punishing Me?

When we go through intense and severe suffering and become disillusioned, negative thoughts seem to stem up from our mind quicker than the positive. I shared earlier how my mind became irrational to the point where I was questioning whether God was punishing me. God however knows and weighs the motives of our hearts as we question Him. He understands and knows us better than we know ourselves. Unless we have an encounter with the God of love remarks such as "God is punishing me" can be uttered by Christians in desperation. Without that encounter, when natural disasters such as earthquakes and hurricanes occur, the world quips that God is punishing people, we may carelessly agree with them. Another time when you may hear such careless comments is when someone is facing inexplicable and prolonged suffering. Those who seem to have the answers to everything are quick to tell the person in trouble that they are being punished by God.

To understand that God does not bring adversity in our lives we must enter into His presence and also taste His love. "Love protects," and because God is love, He protects us from being destroyed by natural disasters or any other troubles. He is a good God who is loving, kind, gracious, full of mercy and goodness. He is not the author of evil but good. I realised God's kind of love can only be understood when we encounter Him. The psalmist also discovered that kind of love by entering into God's presence.

> It was oppressive to me, Till I entered the sanctuary of God, then I understood. (Psalm 73:16–17)

Whenever things become oppressive to us and we begin to wonder about our situation, the first priority is to enter into the sanctuary. There in the sanctuary we will encounter the God who is able to keep us in perfect peace as our mind is steadfast in Him. As we spend time meditating on God's word, and in His presence, then we come to understand not only about His love but what trouble really is. As we are transformed in His presence there is no doubt that our union of love with Him takes a new and higher dimension.

We are not alone in this world and therefore we don't need to be so concerned in figuring out about why things happen. God has revealed all we need to know about trouble. What He will ultimately do one day is bring a complete end to it all. Hence it is important to search the scriptures and be tuned-in to the Holy Spirit. Going deeper in my relationship with God by spending more time with Him and His word, I became aware of love that would never punish. God's love is so pure that as we are drawn to Him it drives us to hunger for more of Him. I believe that all those who desire to go deeper through seeking God more and more will experience that love.

We must be fully convinced that natural disasters do not happen because God wants to punish. The natural disasters are the groanings of the creation according to what we read in the Bible.

> We know that the whole creation has been groaning as in the pains
> of child birth, right up to the present time. (Romans 8:22)

The creation was subjected to frustration and just like us it eagerly waits to be delivered to its original and perfect condition. It is very important that we make a distinction between punishment and discipline, lest we misunderstand the scripture in Hebrews 12:7–11. However, we thank God that He has given us His Holy Spirit who teaches and interprets the word to us. If we are to be transformed in our thinking, it is necessary to keep in step with the Holy Spirit at all times, even when we are reading the Bible.

When our mind is renewed our thinking will be about His pure love, the numerous thoughts that God has towards us, and the good plan which is not for evil. God is not the author of evil, chaos or suffering. He does not sit on His throne asking Himself, "Whom can I punish?" But rather, and here I paraphrase, "His eye ranges across the whole earth looking for anyone in trouble to rescue and strengthen them" (my paraphrase of 2 Chronicles 16:9).

During hard times it is easy to assume that the explanations which seem reasonable to us must be correct, but as we mature in every area of our lives then, our thoughts and speech are changed. We remind ourselves that His thoughts towards us are numerous and good, not evil, and with such a mind we can never accuse or misrepresent Him. Like the psalmist we can enter into the sanctuary, for in His presence the psalmist understood why tough times happened to the righteous. We need to do the same, for only then:

a) We will know that the creation is frustrated and is groaning in pain, because it also desires full redemption, and in its anger and pain it bursts into floods, earthquakes, hurricanes and so forth.

b) We can join with the many Christian organisations, in upholding those affected through prayer and practical support whenever these things happen.

c) We can remind others about the signs and times of the second coming of the Lord. As we lead them to the Lord, they will know Him as their Saviour, and that He never punishes. Jesus said this about the period preceding His second coming:

> There will be great earthquakes, famines and pestilences in various places, and fearful events and great signs from heaven. (Luke 21:11)

Others Say They Are Bewitched or Cursed

Jesus came to bring light into a dark world. As believers, we are not naive or ignorant about that darkness, but at the same time we are aware that we carry the light. We can't read other people's minds but when they speak and express things that are based on their imaginations or worldly belief systems then we can hear the darkness. These are the opportune moments that we can take advantage of and speak the truth in love. As the darkness is dispelled the result is salvation.

I worked with a certain lady—Mercy (not her real name). Over the years we have become great friends, and she is not ashamed to see her story told—for Jesus has changed the story into victory! Whenever she got into any trouble, she believed either her ancestors or people who did not like her were cursing her or bewitching her. She is not alone; there are many others who think the same. Thinking like this in desperate situations and misery can do a lot more harm than good. If you have been thinking like this the scripture below might help you to see things more clearly.

> For it is written "Cursed is everyone who is hung on a tree." (Galatians 3:13b)

My friend however was very serious, and these negative thoughts and beliefs had taken root in her being and become so real to her. What the enemy whispered to her during her difficult times became so real that she believed it, yet it was just thoughts. If we believe that our lives are under the control and outcome of others we are in a more serious kind of trouble which is bondage. When Jesus hung on the cross, He became a curse for us that we may never have to bear it or even live with its effects.

It is God who created us; it is His say over us that counts. Our lives are not controlled by chance of circumstances or what people do to us. We are free of the control of any other power, including that of the enemy. The good news for us is that Jesus is the one in control of our lives as Lord. The choice is ours as to who to believe: people or God?

Jesus has promised us that, "neither death, nor life no demons, no power can separate us from Him," (Romans 8:38) and so we are secure in Him. However, we must be aware that the people who bewitch or curse others are deceived by the devil to carry out his wicked mission. He who is in us is greater than the one in the world and all we need is to rest in that assurance. We are to be transformed by the renewing of our mind in order to know the demonic powers have no grip on those in Christ Jesus. Just in case one is bewitched, as God's children we have been given authority over any bewitching powers and the blood of Jesus covers us. Let us take a moment to remind ourselves what Jesus meant when He said it is finished!

a) To overcome completely, not in part but fully, the power and effects of our troubles, even those we have not yet encountered.
b) To put to finality.
c) To bring to an end.

What a relief that on the cross Jesus had finished, completed, put to finality, brought an end to the works of the devil which included all curses and bewitching. As we read in the Bible, Jesus then sat down at the right hand of God—a sign of the completion of His finished assignment. Today we live in the finished work, the fullness of life that is ours in Christ. We cannot stop people wasting their energy to curse and bewitch us, but all such curses remain ineffective. They only cause us trouble if we worry about them. Our portion is a life of peace and tranquillity in Christ and to walk in love and truth.

The opportunity I had to share the truth of God with Mercy and as she spent time in the word, open to the leading of the Holy Spirit, created a new mindset in her. She now walks in the freedom of her inheritance in Christ, which is as a result of the transformation of a renewed mind. The Bible says:

It is for freedom that Christ has set us free. (Galatians 5:1)

Because she now walks in that freedom whenever troubled times come her way, she is aware that whatever is pure, whatever is excellent and good is what she needs to look for in any hopeless situation. It is beyond our understanding that amid pain and suffering we can express "whatever is excellent," but in Christ the hope of glory, we can. In Jesus, we have hope in every seemingly hopeless situation. Indeed, the same cheerfulness that helped Christ endure the cross is expected of us if we are to share in His glory (Romans 8:17b).

Mercy is now growing in her faith in God, knowing and trusting in Him. The trials of this world are not worth the time, attention and energy that we give them. Jesus wants us to cast them on Him, fixing our attention and directing our energy towards Him instead and the purpose for which He created us. The transformation and growth in Mercy's walk with the Lord encourages me and many who come across her path. When we are truly set free, fruitfulness will be the outward sign of our transformed life. May all, who belong to the household of God grow and glow in the dark places of life.

Pattern of Thoughts

If you are a person who engages with people constantly you might have heard in conversations regarding trouble what I am calling "patterns of thought." They are baseless beliefs people express as a way of appeasing the mind due to the hopeless outlook of their situation. Playing the role of being "our brothers' keeper," is our calling as God's children. So, in a world of superstitions, we need to be aware that sometimes it is a cry for help, and a longing for hope.

One example is when people think they are in trouble as the result of the evil they did in a previous world. Others call it bad luck or a bad omen whenever they are in trouble. These are just imagined thoughts. As we discussed earlier, the earth is the only planet on which God placed humankind. We read in the Bible, that other planets were created to display His power and show His existence, so that we may know Him. God uses many ways to save people and creation is one of them. As we look at the beauty of the sky, the mountains, valleys, the list is endless we are drawn to Him.

> For since the creation of the world- God's invisible qualities—His eternal power and divine nature have been clearly seen, being understood from whatever has been made, so that men are without excuse. (Romans 1:20)

When there is so much suffering others believe that the world is hell, and due to such thinking, they are not open to any positive outcome. They resign themselves to their imaginations and leave things as they are and just get along while they wait to die.

As Christians, we get an opportunity to share the hope we have in Jesus and share the truth found in the word of God. As we share what God says in His word with sensitivity and concern out of love then the pain becomes bearable. But if God uses us as vessels of hope in their hopeless situations, then to Him the glory and praise belongs.

Milk or Solid Food

> I gave you milk not solid foods, for you were not yet ready for it. (1 Cor-3:2)

Paul made this statement to those Christians who were not ready to be fully transformed in their walk with the Lord. We know very well that, during tough times, we are meant to grow. On the other side of the coin we need to be taking solids if we are to withstand tough times. Being led by the Holy Spirit and with the word of God dwelling in us richly, we can understand that the fullness of life that Jesus gives does not exempt us from trouble. That fullness of life is not defined by the presence or absence of trouble. To assume that our life should be smooth sailing all the time with no challenges because we belong to God is a sign that we need milk not solids. The mind that is not yet renewed convinces us that just like our sins were erased so too were our troubles.

We all pass through that milk stage in our walk with God, but we are to keep on growing until we become mature people. Without maturity when we are in troubles, we can become disappointed and that is what brings thoughts that are contrary to what God says about troubles. It is important to remember that suffering comes to us all, Christians and non-Christians. As discussed earlier, our troubles as Christians are greater since we are in opposition with the prince of this world. However, the difference is in the knowledge of what trouble means, where to take it, and knowing who is with us in trouble and that the outcome will be good. When we are transformed by the renewing of our mind, we come out of our milk stage and as we claim God's promises we are certain there will be victory because those promises come to pass.

We shall end this chapter by reminding ourselves of two fundamental truths. Having Jesus as Lord in our lives and being rooted in His word, we will avoid the errors that come from our thoughts. Such beliefs keep us from progression, learning and gain, especially during tough times. Progressively we succumb to despair, frustration, hopelessness and defeat. In tough times we can look for an escape or a coping mechanism and miss the opportunity to be guided to a workable solution of a good outcome.

Prayer

Father, we thank You for the truth of Your word. Renew our minds and protect us from falling into imaginations that are not real. Give us the power and grace to wait patiently for the good You will bring into our situations. Amen.

CHAPTER 3: THREE-FOLD CONNECTION

There is a very familiar story in the Bible, of a man called Job. If you have read his story, then you may understand what I mean by three-fold connection. When we are in trouble it always seems that the person involved is the only one affected. Looking at the account of the story of Job from the scriptures, we discover that others connect with the afflicted person in many ways. The story of Job records unpredicted events of suffering and is one of the most heartfelt stories in the Bible. I will not recite the whole story here but to demonstrate that when troubles come, we are connected in a three-fold dimension.

Job was the person who was afflicted. His wife and friends came when they heard the news and were his constant companions in the days and months that followed. God, the ever-present help in times of trouble, the "Omnipresent" was there too. That is how the three-fold connection is made up:

a) The person in trouble,
b) The circle of friends, family and church family,
c) God.

Each group plays a different role in the situation and I believe we can miss invaluable insights if we concentrate on Job alone as the main player. I have read his story in the past with concern for his suffering and pain without giving much attention to those who were by his side. Therefore, from this paradigm of the three-fold connection, what can we learn as God's children of our role and response, if we are the one afflicted or if we are one of those who come alongside to help, and what is God's position during the tough times in our lives?

Job experienced many of the troubles that we go through, but it seemed strange how it all happened. They came in sequence, one after the other like the gushing rain, which suddenly comes without any warning. Such an experience must have been very confusing and traumatic. It is important to note how Job responded and his attitude to the situation. For it matters so much to God. It also matters to God how the people in our circle respond. In order to clarify that response, I will contrast Job's response to his troubles with the one displayed by the children of Israel when they were in trouble. It is my hope that there are some important lessons for us from Job so that we too may respond in a way that is honouring to God. When his wife wondered how he could continue holding on to God in such suffering, his heart remained pure and painstakingly true.

> His wife said to him, "Are you still holding on to your integrity? Curse God and die!" (Job 2:9)

As I mentioned earlier, we all have different ways of responding and coping with the difficult situations that affect us. The response of those who come alongside us in our times of trouble is important and should not be taken lightly. Job had three friends and his wife beside him during the afflictions. Moses was the one beside the children of Israel in their trouble. God is always also in every situation—the three-fold connection.

The Bible says that whenever the children of Israel got into any trouble God's heart was grieved. I believe their example is recorded for our sake so that we may not fall into the same trap. When Jesus lived here on this earth, He went through a lot of troubles and His response is the best example for us to emulate. He experienced worse troubles than we do because He was taking upon Himself the whole world's troubles—that is why the Bible records Him as a man of sorrows. Unless we take His example and learn to emulate His ways, we too will cause Him grief as the Israelites did. The giants of faith are another good example we can learn from. Whenever they got into trouble, they cried and prayed to the Lord. To cry or call upon the Lord rather than murmur and complain says to God, "I thank You and I trust in You."

In order to understand what it was that grieved God's heart in the way the children of Israel responded to trouble, we will explore their journey from Egypt to the Promised Land. They fussed and were disgruntled about anything and everything and magnified their troubles instead of the One who is greater than all troubles. Our suffering and pain, in combination with our human weaknesses, all contribute to the way we respond. There could still be many other factors which determine our response to trials. It can also depend on the kind of the trouble which we face. Having gone through many troubles, I would be lying to say I haven't travelled the same road many times. Due to God's unfailing love and mercy there is always forgiveness. As the Holy Spirit shows us what is right, we are enabled to respond differently when another trial comes our way. Since they say practise makes perfect, every trial leads us closer to perfection.

The children of Israel encountered many troubles when they left Egypt, but in every situation, God was with them, they were never on their own. Yet for many years, they remained in the state we discussed feeding on milk instead of solid food. Although God was in their midst through trouble after trouble there was no change in the people's response, and so we read that God's heart was grieved. We sometimes take so long to learn, but thankfully God is longsuffering, otherwise no one would escape. He remains the same and because of Jesus then we can view every trouble from an eternal perspective. He is there with us in every trouble and He wants us to take comfort from the fact that He is in control no matter how bad things may seem. As we explore the nature of Israel's response to trouble, we will discover how important it is not to grieve God's heart during our hardships.

Complaining and Murmuring

Complaining and murmuring became a constant and habitual response every time the children of Israel got into trouble. This not only caused grief to the heart of God, it also negatively affected their lives. It became a stronghold, bringing a halt and delay to their progress. They complained and murmured to Moses, but the real issue was that their complaining was indirectly towards God not Moses. It was God who was taking them from Egypt to the Promised Land. Whenever we complain and murmur, we do it to the Lord. God is our creator and He has put us here for a purpose. It is God alone who takes us to the promised destination. Our leaders are only responding to Him in obedience.

God had delivered them from many troubles, and performed many wonders, but thankfulness and trust did not flow easily from their hearts. In their state of dissatisfaction, they expressed a longing to go back instead of going through troubles. 'The good old days' they called them; we too at times express a longing for the good old days when things look bleak.

Job did the same as he spoke of the good old days, but he was not complaining—just remembering. There is nothing wrong in remembering the good old days, but we should never lose sight of the best which lies ahead of us. When we view our troubles from God's perspective, the one who is yesterday, today and forever the same, we will not long for the good old days. Instead we will forget what is behind and keep pressing on for what lies ahead. We must understand that the prospective and the retrospective views together complete our story. Having such a concept keeps us from complaining and murmuring.

To Resign

To resign might not have been an issue with the Israelites, but many of us struggle not to respond to difficulties in this way. We resign and leave the outcome to fate and time, burying our heads in the sand until something happens. This resignation should not be confused with taking away our focus from troubles to focusing on Jesus. When we leave the outcome to an attitude of "whatever" then we have resigned. There are two outcomes in such an attitude, and one is not being engaged with God. The second would be not acknowledging that it is God who has given us a good outcome when it comes. Some will say it is luck or chance, but this is never true for a child of God. Yet even though we know it is God who brings good in any situation, we frequently fail to recognize and give Him the glory due to Him.

Blaming

This is a very common fault, when we shun taking responsibility for our problems and look for someone or something to blame for them. That is what happened in the garden of Eden, where Adam went so far as to blame God for his troubles, even though God had only ever brought him good. Blaming others may provide us with a temporal comfort, but this only brings stagnation as we are not open to any solution. As for the person we are heaping all the blame on, it wears them down too. Eventually, this will bring both parties to a halt and that is what happened to the Israelites and their leader.

Feeling Sorry for Ourselves

The response of feeling sorry for ourselves when we are afflicted, comes in a very subtle way as a result of our fixing our attention and focus on ourselves. We hem ourselves into a pity-party, which is a party for one person alone. The time God has given us to serve and be fruitful is wasted in pity and self-absorption. As the party lingers, it steals our joy and makes us unproductive, robbing us of the desire to get on with our daily chores or engage with God in the situation. We give the troubles too much attention and feelings of helplessness and despair set in.

Advice Seekers

Another common response to affliction is to look for every possible solution from friends, family or church family. This is not necessarily wrong. The concept from the Bible is that we are an integral body. However, turning to our brothers and sisters in Christ without seeking the Lord's counsel is the wrong response. Sometimes we can seek advice, but when it becomes a habit and for every decision and trouble then we need more than advice.

Responding to afflictions in any of the ways I have mentioned above, leads us on a path where we are drawn to ourselves and to others, and that is what happened to the children of Israel. In their response to their troubles they never considered God. God's heart was grieved by this, as it is when we leave God out of our troubles. These responses also cause a lack of joy and disconnection from our life giver. The joy of the Lord is our strength and so unless we draw near to God, we become weak, and the fullness of life that Jesus came to give does not flow through us to the ones around us as God intended.

In the next few pages we will shift from the negative responses to explore how we can respond positively to our troubles in ways which glorify God. Do you remember what Jesus said? "In this world we will have trouble." This means that before we get into any trouble, God sees it coming. He allows it, and He always has a way out; it does not take Him by surprise, neither does He worry about what to do. We are called to be a people of good cheer regardless of what life throws at us. As simple as this solution sounds, to trust and rejoice in God despite the pain and agony, that is the position that becomes our bedrock of hope and security during troubled times. In that position, it is vital to cast our burdens on the Lord and to wait.

From these two words "cast and wait" (eight letters in all) I would like to share how we can respond positively and bring glory to God in times of trouble. It is not a magical formula or a recipe for adventure. This is simply a decision to do what God says, for when we cast our troubles and wait upon Him, He is pleased by such an action. Instead of being grieved, God is glorified through our troubles. As I pointed out at the beginning of this chapter, the three-fold connection is made up of the person in trouble; others, and God, and so we will explore each position in the same order found in the Bible, in the book of Job.

1-The Person Afflicted.

Cast all your anxiety on him because he cares for you. (1 Peter 5:7)

Wait for the Lord, be strong and take heart and wait for the Lord (Psalm 27:14)

God knew that trouble would make us anxious and being anxious affects our lives in many ways which interfere with who we were made to be. As Christians, one of the ways we are distinguished from the rest of the world is by our responses to life's troubles. Anxiety can be identified in somebody's life through their reaction to situations and their words. The Bible says we should be anxious for nothing (Philippians 4:6). When adversity comes, it can trigger a flood of anxiety, worry and tension, but the antidote is prayer and petition, with thanksgiving. That is why it is important as Christians to cast our cares on the Lord if we are to be the witness for Him in a world full of anxiety.

When we cast our cares upon the Lord we are made strong, and instead of anxiety we take heart. It is vital that we respond the right way to the troubles that come into our life. When we respond in the way God desires, those who do not have hope will be drawn to the One who gives us hope, for they will see this hope clearly displayed in our lives. If we are anxious all the time, or when we face trouble, then we are living in defeat not in victory. Though Job's wife and friends thought his troubles had affected his thinking, deep down they could not deny the unwavering trust Job still had in God.

God desires that His children display His splendour daily in every situation, and that includes the tough times, for His purpose is being worked out through our experiences. If we read in the book of Isaiah chapter 53 we will find the answer as to why our troubles can become bearable and that is why Jesus implores us to "cast" all our cares to Him, for he has borne our griefs and carried our sorrows.

Even if you read the Bible repeatedly, you will find no promise that believers will never have troubles. Through the many times I have encountered troubles, I have greatly benefited from meditating on these two simple words: "cast and wait." May God minister to you too as you ponder the insights and raise you out of any anxious thoughts. Jesus is the way of escape from the anxious thoughts that sap our strength and slowly undermine our faith.

Troubles are burdens that weigh heavily on us. To cast requires us to hand them over to the One who came down from heaven and bore our sorrows on the cross. He still stretches out His arms, in readiness both to hold us and carry our troubles. We do this by faith, and then we wait for the Lord to deal with the trouble. We rest in the assurance and peace of knowing He is able to meet our needs. Let us now look at the eight points from the two words (cast and wait).

(C)-Cast

This is an act of faith in God. Faith is the substance on which our relationship with Him is built and the evidence of things hoped for. When we cast our troubles on Him through prayer, faith enables us to release our burdens and stop wearing ourselves down with worry. Take a moment to think of a man who goes fishing. He sits by the lake and casts his fishing line and after that, he sits and waits for his catch. It sounds like an easy example to use but this is exactly what we need to do: "cast." Unlike the fisherman, who is not sure whether there will be any catch of fish, when we cast our burdens on Jesus we know for sure He will carry them for us.

Jesus never fails, that means His side is clear. Then we too must be willing to do just as He says and that is "to cast "and then relax.

Another observation from this picture of the fisherman lies in the patient waiting. If the fisherman reels in his fishing line before catching anything, he would have to look for an alternative meal that day. To cast our troubles to the Lord will always move us towards the need to wait. While we are waiting our attention is no longer on the trouble in our lives but on Jesus.

(A)-Acknowledge

> "Because he loves me," says the Lord, "I will rescue him, I will protect him for he acknowledges my name." (Psalm-91:14)

When we acknowledge God, we are saying He is worthy. Despite the circumstances, He is in control, mighty to save, to deliver and able to change the situation. We are called to acknowledge God in all our ways and not lean on our own understanding. To acknowledge God uses less energy compared to the other options we sometimes turn to when we are in trouble. In our haste to find a solution we frequently lean on our own understanding. This word "acknowledge" is used several times in other places in the Bible but wherever it appears it implies a response. We must respond to our heavenly Father who loves his children and is committed to them and if we acknowledge Him, then we will have the assurance He will never disappoint us. Acknowledging God in our situation opens the way for Him to intervene on our behalf and this is what He promises in the above scripture and many others.

We are God's children, we are no longer our own. Our desire to lean on our own understanding is not a mark of maturity, but a mark of our old nature. As we lay down our will and work with His will, we acknowledge Him and the outcome He promises will be rescue and protection from our troubles. He is gentle and will never interfere with our will. However, He also knows how we are made and therefore never gives up on us. When we acknowledge Him we release control over our troubles to Him, and this is the next step—surrender.

(S)-Surrender

After we have acknowledged God in our situations, we must then surrender ourselves and the situation to Him. This should be total surrender from deep down in our hearts and as we stay tuned to the leading of the Holy Spirit, He gives us the power to lay it all down. As the weight of our troubles has been lifted off our shoulders there is an awareness of relief and peace.

Surrender is the only way that propels us to move towards the good that God desires to bring in our seemingly hopeless situation. Sometimes we drag along, not getting a breakthrough, because we assume that we can handle the minor incidences of trouble ourselves. Surrender must take priority over any notion we have of solving our own troubles, whether big or small, so that we can come to a place where we rely only on God.

Surrender is not a mark of weakness for those who are in Christ, nor is it an indication (as many think) of laxity, complacency or irresponsibility. It is a state of trust and blessed assurance, when our confidence is in God alone. When we are in this state of surrender, we can receive wisdom, direction and insight about what to do with our difficulties. Being in that kind of state enables us to trust in Him who is able. Without surrender it is hard for us to trust, and that is the next step we must take in response to our troubles.

(T)-Trust

Our trust in God is usually formed through a process of seeking Him and desiring to know Him more. As our relationship with Him deepens so our trust in Him increases. It is human nature to trust someone whom we know well in a long-standing and stable relationship. We trust God because of who He is, and because He never disappoints us. We know that He is true and faithful, and we remember that He has never failed us in our past troubles. As we look back to the incidences of His faithfulness, trust should be our only reasonable response. But although God had performed many wonders for the children of Israel, as soon as another tough situation came, they easily forgot His goodness. Yet despite their lack of trust, God remained Faithful.

In our everyday dealings with people we can become disappointed and hurt, sometimes by those who are very close to us, and others who cross our path. This happened to the children of Israel, too. They had been hurt deeply in Egypt. When we have been hurt so deeply, we tread with caution even when we are dealing with the God who loves us, is always there for us, and will never hurt or disappoint us. We can trust Him fully at any time and for anything and therefore there is no reason to be afraid. He gives the same attention and concern for any issue in our lives great or small.

He has never let us down and will never do so. He does not fail and knows all the answers. When He asks us to trust Him to see us through our troubles, He means exactly that. Just like He brought the children of Israel from Egypt to the Promised Land, so has He brought us out too and will not abandon us in the wilderness of our troubles.

I used to walk past a shop and in the shopkeeper's window there was a notice with these words, "where is the man I can trust? For credit—come tomorrow." This notice remained that way as long as that shop remained there. Needless to say, "tomorrow" never came. God's tomorrow, however, *will* come. He is not man and He does not lie. He holds time and is beyond time; the One who knows the future. Jesus gave up everything and even His own life, and so when we cast our cares on Him, we need not doubt or fear; we need not wait for tomorrow. What if our troubles keep us awake at night due to pain or an anxious mind—do we have to wait for daybreak or the following day? The answer is no, for the God who never slumbers or sleeps and neither goes on holiday is our God and we are His people day or night.

If a sparrow does not fall to the ground without our Father's concern, how much more will His concern be for us who are made in His image? Each of us is of more value to Him than the sparrows. Let us trust Him with the small, the big; the significant and insignificant. God's word says, "cast *all* your cares on Him," not some of your cares.

Remember the fisherman, he sits and waits and as he waits, sometimes he can be humming a song—and this leads us to our next point.

(W)-Worship

The strength and desire to worship God do not always come so easily during tough times. Unless we make a deliberate decision to worship, we may find ourselves in despair or discouraged which ultimately leads to depression and finally giving up. Our human inclination is to succumb to what is effortless, and if we pay too much attention to our troubles then worship might feel an effort. We were created to worship

God, and so even when we are weak and have no strength left, the Holy Spirit enables us to worship.

Worship is not a feeling. It is not only done when our hands are lifted high in praise and we are gathered in oneness with God's people. Our outward performance or location does not matter. Our worship flows from the state of who we are in Christ, giving reverent honour to God even when we are in a tight spot and troubles are raging all around. Worship brings out our true self to God. He is worthy of praise and adoration and we worship Him by keeping our focus on Him on a day to day basis. When we are in a tight spot trouble can become a dictator, an intruder which distracts us from focussing on what is more important. I am not suggesting that during difficult times we should refuse to think of our troubles, but rather that dwelling on our problems instead of focussing on our worship to God should be avoided at all costs.

When we portray a positive attitude and remain in expectation and faith for a hopeful outcome, that is worship. Being grateful in our trials, not for them, but because God has not left us to face them alone; acknowledging that He is in control—that too is worship. When we serve others despite the pain; that also is our worship to Him who is worthy.

Job spoke of the greatness of God even amid the intense suffering which can be seen in many of the chapters of his book, and that is the kind of worship we can always offer to God. We see Habakkuk worshipping God in an expression of a tenacious spirit that refused to be defined by what was happening around him. Such a tenacious spirit is worship that diffuses whatever else is within or without. As it flows from the heart and out of our lips, we too like Habakkuk will say:

Yet I will rejoice in the Lord, I will be joyful in God my saviour. (Habakkuk 3:18)

This is a very profound way of demonstrating real worship. It is an example of a lifestyle which is set on pilgrimage. I remember someone giving a testimony of how he was undergoing a very difficult period, but he was hopeful that it would end no matter what. The peace and confidence he displayed could only come from God alone, considering the troubles he was going through. At the end of his testimony, he sang a song, "I will bless the Lord at all times; His praises shall continually be in my mouth." That demonstrated an attitude which said, "It is all about Jesus." In trouble or not, He is worthy of praise, and that kind of response is what was lacking with the Israelites. The response that will not cause grief to God is the position we must choose to take when we are afflicted.

As we rejoice during hardships, blessing the Lord and keeping His praises continually in our mouths, we present a powerful witness to our circle of friends. They ask themselves a question: "how can someone display joy in such hopeless situation?" As they question and wonder, their lives might be affected for good by what they observe from our response. We sometimes preach the good news best with our lives and not with words. When we magnify God instead of our troubles, and as we portray a state of calm, restfulness; joy and peace, that becomes the good news to those in need of salvation.

God is glorified when we worship by giving thanks to His sustaining power and His sufficient grace. I have also observed that at times when we have chosen to worship, the answer to our troubles has come unexpectedly. I have no explanation of how this happens but all I know is that God is good and powerful. He remains constant and unchanging, and He is always thinking about us. Just like He brought down the Jericho walls as his people focused on Him and chose to worship Him amid chaos and uncertainty—so He does today.

On paper, it may sound and appear easy, but it is only possible to worship in difficult times if we understand that we serve the God who commands the waves and storms to be still when raging upon us. Once we know whom we belong to, trusting Him and clinging to His promises that never fail makes the difference. In the momentum of worship, we are led into action. This is a position of motion that leads us to shift our focus from ourselves so that we can serve others. The result is that our attention is no longer on ourselves or the circumstances in our lives.

(A)-Active

As Christians we are called to lead an exemplary life, and when we are going through hard-times, if we don't look for ways that will keep us active, then the troubles dictate our state. We were qualified as overcomers when Jesus cried on the cross, "it is finished!" The finished work of the cross brings a spiritual activity into our lives which is not altered by our afflictions.

To be active in this sense means to shake off passivity and follow the Master in the tasks that need to be done. As we serve God our sole purpose and motive should be for the common good, for unless this is so, eventually our activity can become just something we do to numb our pain. During that time, as God is working on our behalf to bring a good outcome, we must remain purposeful and active too. As we serve others during our interaction with them, we sometimes discover through openness and sharing that their troubles are worse than our own.

Through the sharing and serving, we move from a place of thinking that we are the only ones in trouble and instead our time of interactions become opportunities of learning. Our disappointments and discouragements are turned into lessons through which we change and grow. God uses that time of serving to build us up and to keep us moving in the direction where He is taking us, lest we get stuck in our troubles.

When we are passive and weighed down, as the saying goes, "idleness is the devil's workshop." As children of God we do not want to allow the enemy to make our troubles his workshop. We constantly need to keep reminding ourselves especially in tough times that we are running a race, Jesus is with us all the way and we cannot be derailed by the difficulties in our lives.

Another way to remain active is to stay connected with other believers through fellowship and Bible study. Sickness may restrict our activity even to the point of our being housebound or bed-ridden. When that is the case, willingness to open our homes for prayers with others can help us to stay active. There are times when company is unavailable, yet God remains and our prayers and fellowship with Him is the only active thing to do. God builds and advances His kingdom through us as His co-workers in whatever state we find ourselves in. There are many situations in the world which need God's intervention, and we can play our part in advancing the kingdom through prayer even when restricted by conditions.

Let me suggest another way to divert our thoughts if housebound due to afflictions: reading some good Christian books. I had many books lying on my shelf which I had ignored for a long time but when I was afflicted, they became very handy. It turned out to be an active venture that kept my focus away from trouble and a blessing in many other unexpected ways.

(I)-Inquire

To inquire is to seek the will of God in the situations we find ourselves in, or when we need to make important decisions. When we are in trouble, we easily turn to seeking advice from others. There is nothing wrong in doing that, but though we may feel it is the right thing to do, our first counsel and guidance as children of God must always be from Jesus. He is the One who took our sorrows and is familiar with our troubles. Only He understands and knows the way out. He is delighted when we seek Him first. Inquiring of God, wanting to know what to do, as we take the trouble to Him in prayer is better than running all over asking people for solutions.

Let me give a small illustration; when our cars break down most of us never make any attempt to fix the problem, no matter how small, because we prefer not to mess with it. We accept that we don't have the knowledge and we take it to an expert. In the same way when we are afflicted or needing guidance on a matter, inquiring from the Lord protects us from messing about with our lives. God is always ready when we call and delights to demonstrate His love, care and power. According to the scripture in Isaiah 53, Jesus was marred by our sins, troubles and sorrows beyond description or recognition. He tasted every trouble, knows all things and sees beyond what our eyes can see.

The following are three different biblical accounts of people in trouble and each provides a perfect example of how important it is to inquire of the Lord for any decision in our lives, especially when we are in trouble.

1. At the garden of Gethsemane, in His agony and sorrow, Jesus inquired of His Father what His will was in the situation. He relinquished control into the hands of His Father thus setting an example for us to live by. "Abba Father," He said," everything is

possible for You. Take this cup from me, yet not what I will, but what You will" (Mark 14:36). He inquired "what is your will?"

2. Jehoshaphat was in great distress. He could have gone to seek counsel and advice from his pastor, family, friends or his church family, and it is good to do so, but instead he inquired of the Lord and said:

We do not know what to do, but our eyes are upon You. (2 Chronicles 20:12)

3. David was in big trouble with the Philistines, but he knew the One who knows all the answers and solutions to everything we need.

So David inquired of the Lord, "Shall I go and attack the Philistines? Will you hand them over to me?" (2 Samuel 5:19)

There is an appropriate moment when we can seek counsel from other Christians, especially those that God has placed to be overseers over his flock. God uses innumerable ways which are beyond our thinking to get us out of trouble. Sometimes He does use our brothers and sisters in Christ. His methods however are limitless as everything is subject to Him. There is an incident recorded in the Bible when He even used a donkey to communicate His message (Numbers 22:28). Inquiring from the Lord about what to do when we are in trouble is a good sign that we are trusting in Him alone as the One who is able to bring good into an impossible situation.

When we inquire from the Lord and the answer is opposite to what we expected, we must remember to relate the answer beyond the here-and-now to the bigger picture. When we relinquish our troubles and control of them to God the resulting pay-offs are incredible. In the here and now there is peace, rest, His presence and much more. When we are in such a state of rest and trust, the appropriate timing for telling others comes and we are safe at that time from pressure or confusing advice.

(T) Tell Others

During that time of rest, waiting and inquiring from the Lord, the results could be a direct answer from the Lord. If not we can at such times share the burden with others. If we tell others when we are in a state of rest and knowing God is in control, they are not likely to put pressure on us, urging quick fixes, and so we are not controlled by their expectations. That is the reason why—even if we feel that it is the appropriate time to share what we are going through—we need to exercise wisdom in knowing who the right person is to go to for help. Another danger is that if we get many advisers, we are likely to get conflicting ideas.

Those who will pay attention to what we are saying and just be by our side without necessarily saying or doing anything are more likely to leave a lasting impression. They play a vital role in making a difference in our pain, more so than those who will give opinion and advice which might leave us more troubled than relieved.

Troubles make us vulnerable and sharing with others at the wrong time may do more harm than good. Whoever we choose to share our troubles with, be it those in our fellowship group; a trusted friend, a prayer partner or our church leader, our safe guard is to stay tuned to the leading of the Holy Spirit. Patience and wisdom in waiting for the right timing and choosing the right people is not only a safeguard but also a clear indication that you are not depending on people but on God.

Let's take the example of relationship problems. Unless these are handled with caution and wisdom there could be added heartache. Whether it was shared as a prayer request or just to a friend in confidence. God has called us to be channels of reconciliation and building, since we are in Christ the reconciler. This then means where there is trouble due to broken relationships, we share our pain with others because we are concerned not only of ourselves and our pain but also of those we are in estrangement.

Through troubles we come to know our true friends. These are also times to ask God to give us more grace, love and to shield us from hearing what we do not need to hear. We need to be shielded from hearing those comments that are judgemental and critical, or which offer unhelpful suggestions as reasons for why we are in trouble. Having gone through many troubles many times, I have heard comments such us those of Job's friends: "God is not pleased with you," "you are not praying right," "your faith is weak," etc. Though the enemy used those comments for evil, God however, used the same comments as a tool to shape my character and growth.

Through it all, however, we learn to keep short accounts, by forgiving and not holding grudges over the unwise comments that are made by others when we are going through trials. After all; when we are in difficult situations we have enough to deal with. When such situations occur, we must always remember we may have reacted to others just as unwisely ourselves at times, but God's love and mercy and His power have made us who we are. We also need to be aware that sometimes accusations do not come from the flesh and blood but from the accuser of the brethren. Once we all reach maturity and possess the love of God which is kind, the enemy remains the loser and God's people rise to a new level.

Finally, in your position as you wait upon the Lord your troubles may seem to have gotten worse and you feel like God has abandoned you. Such thoughts are just feelings and feelings are changeable, but the word of God endures forever. God never abandons us. He is forever faithful even when there is no change in our circumstances, we remain hopeful because He is there with us.

The solution is to keep trusting, keep believing, keep praying, and keep rejoicing. Tell yourself that even though you are suffering, and even though you do not understand, you will rejoice in the Lord. People might think you are in denial when you react this way, but you have already got enough on your plate without being concerned about what people might think. Remind yourself that we are all a work in progress, being changed by the potter to think on what is good and excellent. As the potter moulds and changes each one of us, we will become those who encourage and are touched by the pain of others, like Jesus was. Let me conclude that the position of the person in trouble is clearly interwoven with the position of God and others—and so now we turn to consider their positions too.

2-The Position of Others

Going back to Job's account, his wife and a few close friends were by his side during his troubles. We also when we are going through such times have our circle of friends, our church leaders and our family members. It is their position and role that I want to discuss in the next few pages. Just as we have looked at the way God would like us to respond if we are afflicted, He is also concerned about how we respond as we come alongside others when they are in trouble. Feeling concerned about others in their suffering, comes from the DNA of who we are in Christ and how we respond is important to God.

> Carry each other's burdens and in this way, you fulfil the law of Christ. (Galatians 6:2)

Since Jesus carried our burdens, we might ask ourselves, "how do we carry each other's burdens?" To answer this question, we must turn to the word of God. We see how Job's friends did a very good job of carrying his burdens when they just sat and listened. Sadly, when they gave their own advice and opinion, it displeased God (Job 42:7). Just like the person in trouble can grieve God with their response, so can those who come to our aid in times of trouble if they are not led by the Holy Spirit. Our motive and goal must be to carry each other's burdens according to the law of Christ which in summary is to love God above all else and allow His love to flow through us to others. The nature of our role is clearly marked out in this scripture:

> After the Lord had said these things to Job, He said to Eliphaz the Temanite; "I am angry with you and your friends because you have not spoken of me what is right as my servant Job has." (Job 42:7)

Having great ideas, good advice and all the answers for our brothers and sisters while they are in trouble may be good, but it is not what God desires from His children in such situations. Rather, He desires that He should be glorified, and we should be transformed. If the person in trouble is being changed during hardships, we too must sit beside them as Job's friends sat because if God is in our midst, we cannot but be transformed. What we say about God in relation to our troubles can bring life. We should acknowledge His presence in the situation and that He is in control, full of wisdom. It is all about listening and being tuned to the leading of the Holy Spirit. We speak about the greatness of God, of His love for us, of His good plans for us and that nothing is impossible with Him. We too must ask the same question that the person afflicted asks, "God what do You want us to do?" We too must inquire from the Lord to avoid assumption and control.

Where did the friends of Job get it wrong since, when we read Job chapter 22, it sounds like they were speaking right? This is a good reminder to us of how God looks at the heart. We can quote all the scriptures and speak all the right words about God, yet it only comes from our lips, the mental and mechanical aspect. What they did was blow trumpets for themselves. Their advice was based on their own understanding, guess work and personal opinions.

We must be careful when we become concerned by the suffering of others not to forget that God suffered on our behalf and He is more concerned for our suffering than anyone. We are His children and He is a good Father, committed to everything about us. Our human compassion for the sufferer clouds our thinking, making us a stumbling-block to the sufferer as we try to take matters into our own hands. When we do this, despite being well-intentioned, we deprive the sufferer of a chance to experience for themselves the greatness, love and power of God.

We might appear harsh and uncaring but that is not so. We honour God when we refrain from trying to solve other people's problems by our own understanding. Another thing we avoid when we refrain from giving our good advice is the desire to take control, instead letting God be in control of our friend's situation. We should never serve others out of pressure, guilt, self-effort or people's expectations. Rather we serve them so that God may be glorified.

Since we come alongside others to fulfil the law of Christ, we will be blessed with a sense of fulfilment, even though no credit will go to us. Whatever we do it is done unto the Lord. We are a people who are led, no longer doing things the way we used to, but instead bearing each other's burdens. Job's friends failed in taking that position of being burden bearers, but here are some ways in which we can succeed:

Prayer

We read in the Bible, "the prayers of the righteous avail much" (James 5:13–16). Since we are made righteous in Christ Jesus, as we pray for others in trouble our prayers will be effective. It will not be in vain and will not be just another thing to tick off our to-do list. God will answer the prayers that we present to Him on behalf of others.

We pray with confidence because we know God is true to His word, and so our prayers are based on God's will for the person in need. God's will for every one of us is to become more like Jesus.

Hardships shape and test a person's faith, so we could pray for them to be given strength and endurance, and that they will remember God's grace is sufficient for them. We could pray like Jesus prayed for Peter, that their faith will remain strong and that they do not give up. Such prayers are always valid, even if we have not been given a specific request or we have not heard from the Holy Spirit.

God's answer to our prayers may not be seen or be experienced immediately. If this is the case, we must avoid counteracting our prayers with negative speaking due to our desire to see our friend delivered quickly from suffering. If the answer is delayed, since we have prayed, and He knows what is best for His children, we leave the request and outcome to Him in His hands. As we pray and listen to the Lord, He may sometimes choose one of His children as a channel through which He brings the answer. I will expound on this using an example of a friend of mine who was one time praying her usual prayers. She was unaware of what I was going through, but God knew and He spoke to her instructing her what to do on my behalf.

I was in a very difficult situation at that time—I had prayed, and as months passed by, until I became weary of praying. The prolonged waiting upon the Lord due to despair led me into a state of isolation. I cut off and lost all contact with many people. Sometimes when we are pushed into a corner by what is happening in our lives, we cut off contact from others, not intentionally pushing others away, but because we retreat inside ourselves. Sometimes the repetition of our troubles wears us down, and the enemy receives too much attention. Therefore, we opt for the easiest way available to us—which most of the time is isolation.

God is always thinking good thoughts towards us, and though troubles do isolate us from others—we are never out of His reach and eye. I was not aware that He was thinking good thoughts about me until my friend called unexpectedly, and said, "God says you are in a storm." Most assuredly I was, and I couldn't deny it. Following that remark, a long conversation ensued which led to a miraculous door opening instantly. It was the kind of sudden moment miracle which without a shadow of doubt could only come from God.

Within a period of two weeks I was up and running and walking in God's goodness, unspeakable joy and blessings. I was glad that I had maintained the same phone number otherwise my friend might not have reached me. In reality, I'm sure God would have reached out to me somehow, He knows where we live, our postcode and our telephone number! He knows everything, and nothing is hidden from Him.

What am I saying? We are co-workers with the master of the universe. When we pray, our prayers become the vehicle through which we do business with God. He is the One who sees those in trouble and knows all the things which are hidden from our sight. As we keep our spiritual ears open to Him during our prayer time, just like He hears our requests we too will hear where He wants to send us.

Practical Support

We should never take for granted the power of serving in simple practical ways as a demonstration of God's love in action, giving up our time and schedules to stand beside someone in trouble. As I think of the results, I am reminded of how Rachel (not her real name) was overtaken by grief. Her beloved mother had gone home to be with the Lord and her grief was unbearable. Simple and important tasks we do every day became neglected. The pile of unwashed clothes and other household tasks that were left unattended were an indication of the extent to which her grief which had taken away her strength to do such tasks.

However, a few people from God's family where she attended church noticed she had missed meetings for some time and they planned to visit her. From their visit a plan of action for practical help was arranged. This loving family of God visited regularly; they sat and helped with household chores, shopping; taking the children out and preparing meals for the family. Gradually with prayer, a listening ear, practical help and encouragement, her grief took the healthy process which is a necessary part of God's way of healing. Her hope started to rise, and she resumed attending church and was up and running the race once again.

We like doing good deeds for others because that is who we are, endowed with a servant heart by the God who came from heaven to serve. As we reach out with sensitivity and wisdom, open to the leading of the Holy Spirit, we avoid repeating the mistakes made by Job's friends. While there are many ways in which we can help our brothers and sisters during their trials, as we serve them, we must be careful not to burden ourselves in the process.

Practical help demonstrates faith without works is dead. It also fulfils the law of love. However, as I stated earlier, some troubles can cause damage deeper than any human eye can see. Therefore, as we serve, we bear in mind that for complete wholeness only God can fix the broken pieces. Because of that brokenness, caution, wisdom and sensitivity are needed as we offer our help. Practical help from the right motive will enable the person in trouble to divert their mind and attention from what surrounds them. It creates an opportunity for them to take stock and reflect, while at the same time they experience a touch of God through our service.

Practical help demonstrates the reality of what it means to be the body of Christ, a people who are united because they belong to one Father. We see this example demonstrated by the early church as we read from the Bible:

> All the believers were one in heart and mind. No one claimed that any of his possessions was his own, but they shared everything they had. There were no needy persons among them. For from time to time those who owned lands or houses sold them, brought the money from the sales and put it at the apostles' feet and it was distributed to anyone as he had need. (Acts 4:32–35)

In the above example, the burden of financial troubles being experienced by some believers was lifted in a united effort. For the church of Jesus Christ in our day, if we are to be complete in every good work, united in a common goal for the glory of God, then seeing the bigger picture is crucial. If we are one in heart and mind, with one Father, faith, love, hope, and purpose, then our help will be effective, and God will not be grieved by how we respond to those in trouble.

Encouragement

Another thing we can do is to encourage those in trouble. For some of us, encouraging others seems to flow naturally as this too is a gift from God. He is the One who encourages us on our journey, when we feel like we cannot continue or bear much longer. He sends others to us to do the same.

You hear oh Lord the desire of the afflicted, you encourage them, and you listen to their cry. (Psalms 10:17)

We are clothed in Christ; therefore, we encourage with what has already been deposited within us by the Lord Himself. We can build and uplift, bringing a new and hopeful determination for the person in trouble. Rachel was restored to newness of life because the motivating factor with those who helped her was love. Where the motive is wrong, pity for example, the person may feel a sense of defeat and hopelessness. Then other feelings may creep in; even powerlessness can take over, which leads to self-pity and a worse outcome is created.

Using examples in the word of God and what He has deposited within us protects us against the temptation to assume a position of elevation, control or putting pressure on the afflicted person. We are also freed from feelings of frustration and limitation that we have not done enough or that we have nothing to offer our brothers and sisters in trouble. As we remind them of the promises of God, of how He never fails, of how He loves and values them, and that gives them courage to stay on track.

Another powerful tool in encouraging others is when we share a testimony. A testimony tells others of miracles that have already taken place in our lives, not second-hand tales but our own story of how God brought us through our afflictions. Since such testimonies are birthed out of our adversity, they are a powerful witness.

All the miracles Jesus performed were for people in trouble: the sick, the poor, the bereaved, those facing natural disasters such as shipwreck, and others. When they cried to the Lord, He delivered them from all their troubles and a testimony was birthed. Thus, our troubles become the very tool God uses to encourage others. Sometimes we shy away from sharing our testimonies and we keep all these victories to ourselves, yet they are meant to bring glory to God, and uplift those in trouble.

A testimony is also a sure way of keeping us in a safe position of not adding any injury or more heartache to the seemingly impossible situation as it will only testify of what God did in our situation. Where we have no testimony then being there beside our brothers and sisters is of greater value than we can ever imagine. When we have done all that we can do and have nothing else to say we must be honest to accept that we do not know or understand but God does. We must always remember that we can give encouragement just through listening and being beside the person. This matters more to God, and the person in trouble, than words. When Jesus and his disciples were in the Garden of Gethsemane, their presence with Him was more important. They did not even pray for they had been overtaken by fatigue and grief but despite that, they were there.

Listening Ear

The art of listening is a very important aspect of who we are as God's children. God wants us to be a people who listen not only to Him but to others. He wants us to be there and ready to listen when their hearts are crushed by trouble. To listen we must slow down and exercise patience. Having a patient character makes listening come easily. We live in a very fast world where we are always conscious about time. You and I know that patience is a powerful gift from the Holy Spirit and we all need it, not only when dealing with others but in our own lives as God's people. I have learned that many of the mistakes I make are due to lack of patience. When God gives me a promise, my patience runs out if the promise is not fulfilled within my expected timing.

I have observed that my prayer times too can also be hurried by to-do lists, and just like I leave the throne room in a hurry, I can bring the same attitude to those who are hurting and are in need. Slowing down to listen rather than giving advice to someone when they are going through tough times is a treasure to them, which we miss due to lack of patience.

Exercising patience and paying attention through listening to others in trouble not only benefits the one in trouble; through the process our character is also changed. We live in a world where the clock ticks louder than the voices of those who matter and are within our reach. Without paying much attention to what they are saying, or feeling their deep heartfelt expression, we find ourselves quick with a ready-made solution and answer. As we listen to the clock and look at our busy schedules, we miss that "now" moment. However, God never fails; our times are in His hands and He always brings another opportunity for us so that we can do what is right.

The eyes of the Lord are on the righteous and His ears are attentive to their cry. (Psalm 34:15)

If we follow His example, the clock will still tick but the other way around. The voices of those who matter will be louder and clearer. Just like His ears are attentive to our cry, we too need to show the same attentiveness to others and to Him, if we are willing to listen. He speaks and gives clear instructions on what to do in the situation or what not to do. Sometimes He speaks in that still small voice, other times, an impression, or just the peace of His presence. Whatever method He uses His ear is attentive to our cry for He is forever faithful to us, His children.

If being slow to speak and quick to listen is what is required of us (James 1:19), then if listening is all we can offer those in trouble, it is an invaluable gift. Job was in such pain and agony, that all he would have wished for was someone to sit there beside him, who would be slow to speak but quick to listen. Unfortunately, his friends never realised what was needed. While someone is in such agony and pain, their greatest desire is to know that someone is walking with them. It gives them comfort as they explore the pathway of the tough times which they find themselves in, and that makes a big difference.

When Jesus approached people in difficult situations, He never used the same method to bring about a good outcome. Sometimes He prayed, at other times He gave various instructions what to do. However, the greatest moment for them was when He listened and stopped to pay attention. As He showed concern the effects went deeper. We will do the same if we follow His example. Also, we remain in a safe position where we will not have any regrets later or a response that grieves God.

3-God's Position

Understanding God's position is crucial if we are to live in the victory of the finished work of the cross even in times of extreme difficulties. He is the present help in times of trouble, but His presence does not only affect the afflicted but us all. His blessings overflow to all and as He intervenes in our situations even those who thought they had no need are made aware of their spiritual poverty. The friends of Job may have thought that they had no need, but God knew better.

Both parties came to a point of knowing that God is always there to hear our conversations. As Job was restored, his friends too were taken to another level of understanding the love of God, His mercies, grace; His faithfulness and His power to change the impossible. The ever-present help in trouble brings wonderful effects to the afflicted and those who come alongside us.

It is likely that when our suffering is so intense, and especially when it lingers on and on until we sink into despair and a helpless state, we can drift into moments of wondering "what's the point?" To overcome during these moments we need to understand the position of God and remember that our Saviour cried out in agony, "not my will but your will be done." Whatever kind of trials we face, and no matter how hopeless the situation looks, it is paramount to remember God is in it too and we are not alone. He is there to see us through, to give us strength and keep us from giving up.

In trying to explore God's position, we want to remind ourselves of what we know about Him, His character and what He does. When everything is falling apart in our lives, God is the steadfast anchor when the storms of life are raging upon us, and they cannot destroy us because we are in Him. As we discover these wonderful truths of His position, then we know how secure we are even in seasons of adversity.

God is in Control

> In the beginning, you laid the foundations of the earth and the heavens are the works of your hands. They will perish but you remain, your years will never end. (Psalm 102:25–27)

What a powerful assurance that we desperately need to hear when we are in trouble! We need to allow it to settle deep into our inner being without a doubt. Everything is subject to wear and is coming to an end—including our troubles. Gladly our God remains the same, unshakable and in control of the whole universe. So, if the universe itself will wear out like a garment, then our own troubles which are equally temporal must soon wear away and ultimately be removed when we all get to heaven, when Jesus will bring all suffering to an end and will make all things new. So, whether our deliverance comes here and now or when the end comes, we can still go through tough times with a heavenly peace as conquerors.

Since we know that God is in control, even though troubles may surround us, the One in control of the universe surrounds us too. He gives us the assurance that we are secure, and nothing can separate us from His love. He is in control not only of our lives but even the circumstances that beset us. This knowledge gives us peace from within which is not affected by what is without. We remind ourselves that God is in control and not the trials we face in life. We take hold of the truth that He is bigger than our troubles and are fully persuaded that we are secure in Him. He is our strength, our comforter; refuge, our hiding place and our shelter in the storms of life.

It is important to remember that although humans fell into sin, God was not affected by the fall and therefore His position remains. It is a position that is unchangeable and never shaken. When seeming chaos prevails all around us, there is a common question many people ask: "What is God doing or can't He do something?" They ask this question especially when there is a natural disaster. The disciples asked the same question when their boat was tossed by the waves, but the Master was not affected by the waves and as they woke Him up they asked Him, "Teacher, don't you care if we drown?" Shortly after, they realised He was in control as He quieted the storm (Mark 4:38–41).

would have been good to give examples

As we reflect on the expanse of the universe, we can never deny that God is in control. As we read the stories of the difficulties which giants of faith have encountered, and how God rescued them, we too will acknowledge that, "God is in control." He demonstrated His position in the hardships of those who have gone before us. He is above all power and He is in control and that is His position forever.

When relationships break down, He is the friend who sticks closer than a brother. When hearts break, He is the One who heals the broken pieces. When others reject you, He is the Father who accepts you just the way you are and will never reject you. When sickness strikes, He is our healer. In grief and loss, He is our comforter. In loneliness, He is our companion. When natural disasters destroy all that we hold dear; He gives hope for a new beginning. Where we have financial troubles, He is our provider and when we need safety, He is our hiding place. His position is that of being more than enough for us whatever comes our way.

God is All-Wise and Powerful

Throughout the scriptures God reveals to us another aspect of Himself. Not only is He in control but He is also wise, powerful and knows the future. As we said earlier not one of our troubles takes Him by surprise, He knows them before they happen. We can therefore be encouraged to know, the next time we find ourselves in difficulty, that God is aware. His position is never affected by our search for answers or our doubts. Sometimes when we are suffering, we wonder "what is God doing?" The answer unfolds as we see His power demonstrated in the situation.

This power became visible to the disciples when they were wondering what God was doing as the waves raged upon them. They were rescued from their troubles, freed from their fears and they got the answer to their questioning minds. He is more powerful than anything we can ever encounter; all we need to do is to believe and trust. This simplicity comes as we move from the natural realm and from our own understanding to acknowledge that He is powerful and wise. The power and wisdom of God available to us is His creative power. God does not run out of solutions, for He is able to bring into being that which does not exist. The Bible tells us that He calls those things that are not to be as if they were (Romans 4:17b). That is our assurance that if at any time we feel all our resources, answers and solutions are exhausted, with God there is always a possibility of creativity. There are times He averts trouble from us as He sees it coming when we are not even aware of it. Sometimes He averts it, but He lets us see how He has intervened in situations that could have destroyed us.

Jesus is Always With Us

God has said He will never leave us or forsake us, therefore even when we are in trouble, He is with us. Feelings can deceive us, so we must refuse to go by how we feel. This means moving from listening to our feelings to believing in our hearts, that Jesus is with us in trouble and will never leave us or forsake us. He walks with us through it all, as he was with the disciples at sea in the storm. Think of Joseph in Egypt, how he went through trouble after trouble and yet through it all God's hand was evident in the circumstances. He was present in the unseen and will never leave or forsake His own. Because of the indwelling presence of God, hard times in our lives must be laid down so that the

God who is great and bigger than our troubles is seen as He is, and His position remains the same forever.

Whatever trouble comes our way, God's presence gives us peace that our human understanding cannot explain. It is the peace that passes all understanding. I experienced this peace when my beloved brother went to be with the Lord. I found myself in a very dark place, but even in that darkness there was a tangible peace that made me aware that Jesus was with me. The comfort we all desperately need in times of loss is available from Jesus. He is an ever-present Help when we desperately need someone with us.

He knows when we need an urgent intervention and as we shift our focus from our troubles, we realise He is right there with us. The best way to stay focused is to recall how He has brought us through before, and to look at examples of situations of others known to us. What of those giants of faith? With all these examples the evidence of where we can find God during the tough times is clearer than our perception. He is right there with us. We have no record of Him ever failing anyone, and since we have a better covenant of, "Emanuel, God with us," that is our bedrock of our hope.

God's Promises are True

Another thing that we can be sure of during trouble is that God's promises are unchangeable. His promises are true and real, just as real as His power and wisdom and His presence. It is one thing to know His promises never fail, but unless we own them as our inheritance, and believe and receive them, they remain like a gift on our shelf that is never opened. We are called to be a people who live by the word that comes from the mouth of God in every area of our lives. God's word brings life in every trouble—and we need to move on from knowing this in theory, to seeing it happen in our lives according to His will.

> For no matter, how many promises God has made they are "yes" in Christ, and so through Him "Amen" is spoken by us to the glory of God. (2 Corinthians 1:20)

Just as salvation is freely given, but one must receive it by faith, so are His promises. It is like being given a cheque by someone. If one does not cash the cheque, the money remains in the bank. Where do we cash the cheque and how? Our manual, the Bible, is full of inexhaustible promises for whatever we need. The following promise given by Jesus does not set any limits to what we can ask for, in good and bad times:

> If you remain in me and my words remain in you, ask whatever you wish, and it will be given you. (John 15:7)

For every trouble and for anything else that we need in this life this scripture is conclusive. He lacks nothing, and therefore His promises are for us not for Himself. Once we claim them, He always honours His word, but we must also remain in Him. Sometimes God drops His promises in our heart through the scripture or with just a whisper. In whatever way the promise is given, all we must do is believe and claim it, for whatever the need may be. Remain in Him and let His words remain in you then, "ask." Many of us have been through tough times, and at the time we could not see any way out in the natural. We came through because God is faithful and committed in fulfilling His promises.

While Job was in agony he understood that God was true to His promises, which are "Yes and Amen," and to affirm his "Amen" he said:

> He performs wonders that cannot be fathomed, miracles that cannot be counted. (Job 9:10)

There are many times when, due to the pressures of life, we fail to keep the promises we make to other people. We sometimes forget that we even promised. We can count on God because He always fulfils what He has promised. Therefore, we need to keep trusting the One who does not make empty promises. When He gives a promise then we receive it and live in a state of expectation no matter how pressed by trouble we may be, until it comes to pass.

Prayer

Our heavenly Father, we thank You that You are in control of the universe. We pray that Your Holy Spirit will remind us that You are always with us in trouble. We thank You that we can stand on every one of Your promises with the assurance that in Jesus they are "Yes and Amen."

CHAPTER 4: EXPECTING GOOD OUTCOMES

In the morning, I lay my requests before you and wait in expectation. (Psalm 5:3b)

After screaming, fighting, fretting, rebuking the enemy and quoting every scripture because of our troubles, especially when they linger for a long time, we become weary. However, whatever strength and flicker of hope is still left it is important to maintain an attitude of expectation. There is a promise for those who love God and are called according to His purpose—hence the reason why we expect a good outcome. Another benefit of expecting a good outcome will be stillness and thus the weariness does come to an end. As we remember the scripture, how God turns what was meant for evil into good, then we will be prepared to receive. Like the psalmist, we wait in stillness and expectation. For when we are still it becomes easy to hear from God.

I remember one Christmas my sister called to inform me that she had bought a gift and had put it in the post. I looked forward to the postman knocking at my door any time. I was expecting the promised gift from my sister in the coming days or weeks. I waited patiently, and I was not anxious and neither did I put everything on hold. I continued with my daily chores as usual. I knew that my sister would not lie to me and I trusted and believed that she would keep her promise to me. She had purchased the gift and I was eager and looking forward in expectation.

We may wait in expectation even when no one has promised any gift when we know it is a season of goodwill. But when we have not been promised beforehand, we may not be so certain or eager and there may be no guarantee that someone will give us a gift. I knew without a shadow of doubt this gift was coming and because of the relationship I have with my sister I trusted her. In a similar way, since we are God's children, and know without any doubt that He can be trusted to give what He has promised, then we wait in expectation. God's promises never fail, and He says, "I will turn your mourning into dancing" and when we are in trouble, He whispers, "The troubles you are going through I will turn them into good."

What I have said, that I bring about, what I have planned that will I do. (Isaiah 46:11b)

What did He say, and what did He plan? That in Jesus Christ we are more than conquerors; that the righteous may have many troubles but the Lord delivers us from them all. Our attitude of expectation is very important for it protects us from despair and keeps us focused on what God has promised. I would like us to look at four ways of doing that.

An Attitude of Praise and Trust

Habakkuk was saddened by the injustice he saw in his day, something which is sadly still common today. He struggled to understand, and he was very disturbed about it to the point of writing a letter to God. He had no answers and could make no sense of all the injustice he saw. Although he had no answers and felt helpless, he chose to trust in the One who knows all things and who brings good out of every hopeless situation. His attitude of expectation and trusting in God is what he demonstrated in the situation of the injustice.

There are three things that Habakkuk reminded himself of in expectant stillness before God:

1) God is in control, "sun and moon stood still in the heavens at the glint of your flying arrows" (Habakkuk 3:11).
2) Trusting God for intervention, "Yet I will wait patiently for the day of calamity" (to the enemy) (Habakkuk 2:16b).
3) He had faith in God, "But the righteous shall live by his faith" (Habakkuk 2:4b). He did not define the situation according to his five senses. He saw the outcome and lived by faith and expectation while he waited to see God's intervention.

The result in meditating and knowing what God can do led him to a state of stillness and peace in anticipation of a good outcome. He had not seen it and his circumstances were still the same. There is no record of how long the injustices lasted. All we know is that he saw a good outcome by faith and knew that God would intervene in the situation. He refused to put his life on hold. He continued to serve, loving God and others and giving God the glory despite his troubles.

Remembering the Past Miracles of God

I will remember the deeds of the Lord; yes, I will remember your miracles of long ago. I will meditate on all your works and consider all your mighty deeds. (Psalm 77:11–12)

Unlike Habakkuk, the above scripture implies that when we are in trouble, another way of expecting a good outcome is by reflecting and remembering God's mighty deeds in the past. Therefore, whatever circumstances the writer was in at that moment, the fact that he reminded himself of the past miracles of God is a sign that he was expectant. He considered how mighty God's deeds have always been, mightier than the troubles he was facing. He was fully convinced that God is the One who performs miracles in our hopeless situations. Such an attitude of reflecting and reminding ourselves of the wonders of God is vital if we are to retain the hope of a good outcome.

While we are waiting for a good outcome, we need to tell our souls about the past victories that God has brought us through. These past miracles will encourage us in the present, for although we have been through many trials, we have been delivered from them all. As we note in the above scripture, the focus is not in remembering or reflecting on how we have suffered in the past, but on the goodness of the Lord. As we remember the miracles of long ago, the wonders of the Lord God Almighty, in the face of our troubles then our expectation of a good outcome is fuelled and sustained.

We must let go of the past in order to embrace the future. Therefore, when we are hemmed in by troubles and our mind wanders back to some painful incidents the thought must be captured. Our focus and expectation must only be of the wonders of God and the good outcome we expect Him to bring.

Even as we look forward to the good outcome that God has promised, it is important that we wait in expectation. We could sometimes wait so long that we begin to abandon any expectation of good, but God always fulfils His promises to us. He remains committed to see us through because He always finishes what He begins.

Breaking Down Dividing Walls

Anger; bitterness, resentment and unforgiveness are not mere words, but barriers that become dividing walls which sometimes block God's answers to our prayers. We may sometimes think God is not answering our prayers, while the problem is always some hindrance on our part. I experienced this one time when my heart was full of bitterness. As I prayed it felt like heaven was shut; but heaven is always open. God is full of mercy and He loves to give good gifts to His children. He does not withhold any good thing from us. Whenever at any time we may feel like heaven is shut, we should consult with the Holy Spirit for the reason.

Whatever the Holy Spirit highlights, if we want a good outcome for the situation then we must bring down any wall between us and God so that our prayers are not hindered. It is no wonder that we are commanded in the Bible to get rid of these barriers (Colossians 3:8). We are the ones who must destroy those walls completely without hesitation. When we have been deeply hurt and harbour any of the above offences, they become dividing walls. We constantly cry to the Lord when we are in trouble for Him to answer and God hears us because He loves us so much. He also promises to answer when we call, and He does just as He has promised. The answer, however, may be held back by a wall we have created between us and those we are estranged from. Though our hands are ready and open to receive, our hearts are often not ready.

Therefore, as we take stock of our lives, and deal with these barriers, we are preparing ourselves for a good outcome. When my sister called to say she had sent a gift through the post, I cleared my cupboards of any clutter to make space for the gift. In the same way it is crucial that we get rid of any barrier by acknowledging it to God and seeking His mercy and forgiveness. Once we break down the walls, and the way is clear the answer comes through.

Let's bear in mind that God always delights in our prayers, and that He answers whenever we call. His love for us is never affected by those walls.

The following testimony is a very profound example of what sometimes happens when these walls are not broken as we seek the

Lord for intervention in our afflictions. A man was in his late 40s and had been suffering from high blood pressure. He was in a strained relationship with his Dad and was full of anger and resentment towards him for quite some time. He had big trouble and had to spend some years visiting the doctors and taking pills regularly.

One day as he prayed about his healing, he felt the Lord was speaking to him about his relationship with his Dad. He asked the Lord to forgive him of his bitterness and anger towards his Dad. From there he made a choice to follow what he felt God was saying and did the right thing. He acted by breaking down a wall that not only separated him from his Dad but also had blocked his answer from His Heavenly Father. They were reconciled and after some months he recognised his sickness had completely gone.

The man took stock of his walk with God during his troubles and obeyed what he felt led to do by God's still small voice. His next step was to break down the wall of bitterness, resentment, and un-forgiveness which hindered his relationship with his father. When we are in trouble, we must take it to God in prayer, to cast it upon Him and tune into His leading and act accordingly and in expectation.

For every trouble and for each individual God is the One from whom no secret is hidden. We should never guess or compare ourselves with another person's reason why our prayers have not been answered. Whatever the Holy Spirit reveals to us as we pray during the tough times is very personal and specific according to our need. Responding and acting on what has been revealed is what matters.

Speaking Words of Life

Finally, we need to be careful with regard to what we say about the troubles that we are in. We all know that God spoke creation into being and as His children we too should always speak life in our situations. If we have been saying in cases of sickness, "this sickness will never get better," or "my financial situation will never improve," then we must instead begin to speak what God says. When we are hard pressed, we need to shut off and refuse to listen to negative voices or live by sight. This demonstrates that we are an expectant people, co-workers with the Master as He turns that which was meant for evil into good.

Prayer

Father we thank You that You are in control and You turn what the enemy meant to destroy us into good. Holy Spirit help us to live our life expecting a good outcome out of our afflictions. In Jesus' name we ask. Amen.

CHAPTER 5: THE GOOD OUTCOME

And we know that in all things, God works for the good of those who love him, who have been called according to his purpose. (Romans 8:28)

What stands out clearly in this scripture is that those who are called in Christ are living and walking in God's purposes through good times and bad. When we are at ease without any troubles, it is because of what Jesus accomplished on the cross, and of the fulfilment of His promises. When we are surrounded by troubles and our suffering is unbearable, we must remember it is only for a little while. We are also privileged to be those who will share in His glory. Either way, we are walking in victory and this is the purpose we were created for—to display the glory of God.

While we are going through a lot of trouble we wonder when and how it will ever end. According to the above scripture, whatever life throws at us, God always brings good out of our troubles. If trouble does not come to an end, even if this text is not immediately fulfilled for us in the here and now, we still have the certainty that our trials will ultimately come to an end one day when we get to heaven. There the good outcome will be permanent. God fulfils every word He has spoken and though we may not see the good outcome at the present time but rather experience pain and distress, a good outcome will eventually come.

After all that Job had to bear, his suffering came to an end and everything was restored in a good outcome. Joseph came out of the pit, out of Potiphar's house and, out of prison into a glorious outcome. We too in our day have been through tough times and we have come out victoriously because Jesus always leads us in triumphant procession. For those who are in Christ, the outcome of our afflictions is good here and now, and they will end completely when we get to heaven. Hidden within the suffering is always something good for those who are called according to His purpose.

As I was going through my own troubles my eyes were opened to eight good outcomes. These outcomes are just a small fraction of the many wonders that God performs every day in good or bad times. I hope and pray that whenever you are faced with situations on your journey to heaven that do not show any signs of a good outcome, remind yourself that God performs wonders. The good outcome, however, must not be interpreted according to our understanding—otherwise we will become frustrated instead of recognizing God's wonders. In order to avoid being disappointed with the outcome that God brings in our situations, our perception should align with His. Let us now look at the eight outcomes. Our trials are meant:

To Give Knowledge and Understanding

This is knowledge that comes from God. It is unlikely to be found elsewhere. It gives us understanding of who He is, His ways; who we are and of life in general. God gives us understanding through His Spirit and through His word of why bad things happen and His ultimate plan to bring all suffering to an end. In the book of Job (chapters 38–39) God gave Job that knowledge and understanding in a fresh way while he was suffering. Our suffering is never wasted—there is always a good outcome.

When we understand, we move from despair to hope, from lethargy to strength, and from restlessness to peace. When the eyes of our understanding are opened, we can take heart next time any trouble comes. As we see our troubles from a higher viewpoint, we become a people of good cheer even when there is no change in our circumstances.

As long as we are on this side of eternity and before the second coming of our Lord, adversities will come, but as God gives us knowledge and understanding we can take courage and respond in a different way from the people of the world. The emphasis of the above scripture that the evil will be turned into good is only for those who are called according to God's purpose.

One of the greatest threats to the enemy is our call and he will throw every trouble or whatever it takes to side-track us from fulfilling that call. But if we focus on Jesus and not on our troubles we will stay on the right track. As we spend time in His presence and meditate on his word, the outcome will certainly be that we receive knowledge and understanding for He is the best Teacher for any subject, including affliction.

For Character Building

Not only so, but we also rejoice in our sufferings because we know that suffering produces perseverance, perseverance, character; and character, hope. (Roman 5:3–4)

It is always helpful to remember that while suffering is unpleasant, yet for those in Christ it always serves a purpose. We often look at trouble in a negative way, because it interrupts our comfortable plans. Sometimes even our lives can be destroyed. The truth of it all is that God develops our character during our afflictions. He is the One who has good plans for us, therefore, we do not need to worry about our plans being interrupted.

As we persevere and are fully depending upon God then we no longer need to rush the process of waiting. We will no longer desire to manipulate our way out of trouble through quick fixes. Instead we allow perseverance to finish its work. Our human nature is weak and subject to giving up, or to look for quick fixes, but God gives us strength to persevere. As those who are predestined, giving up is not an option—rather our option and goal is to keep pressing on towards the hope of a good outcome, in this case the formation of our characters. When God takes over, He can use our troubles for our absolute deliverance into new beginnings and character growth. It is Him who makes all things beautiful, taking even the broken and shattered pieces of our lives as He builds our character. As we allow God to tear down and build our lives using troubles, then in the process we become more like Jesus. All of us would desire to embrace with all our heart such an outcome.

I once heard a story about a wealthy lady on the ill-fated Titanic, how after she secured a place in the life boat she decided to go back to her cabin. She found the floor littered with her beautiful gems, bank notes and three oranges. One look at all these items and what she chose to retrieve were the three oranges and went back to the waiting boat. This tragedy transformed her values and clarified her priorities. As our character is changed during trouble, we realise more clearly what is important, and from there we start to hold onto the things of this world loosely—and that is a good outcome. Through our upward journey, every day can bring something along the way—a hardship which God can use to mould our character. As our character is developed the result is the fruit of the Holy Spirit.

> But the fruit of the Spirit is love, joy, peace, patience; kindness; goodness, faithfulness; gentleness and self-control. (Galatians 5:22)

To become like Jesus, we must possess the fruit of the Holy Spirit. A fruit is visible, very appealing to the eye and nourishing to our bodies. When Jesus lived here on earth people were drawn to him because they saw every quality of the fruit of the Holy Spirit. He desires the same for us—that as we grow in character to be like Him the benefit is for the world around us. As God is glorified as we become like Him, we inherit the good Jesus came to give us, and those in the world may ultimately receive salvation. Here are a few examples of what the fruit of the Spirit looks like.

Love—Is demonstrated as we move from self-focus to caring and serving others despite of our troubles. Remember the story of the woman on the Titanic. She took and shared the oranges with her fellow passengers in the life boat. She was no longer concerned for herself or her silver and gold, but about the people who were with her in the boat. She demonstrated how to love your neighbour as yourself.

Joy—The living hope gives us a joy that wells up from within to the outside. It causes sadness, despair and sorrow to melt away and as people see that joy, we become a witness to those around us that even in trouble joy can never be hindered. As people watch and see that those in Christ react differently to troubles, they are attracted by such a life and they too will want to respond to the giver of such joy.

Peace—We are at rest in our inner selves and cannot be tossed, like waves in the sea and that peace takes over any anxious thoughts. Jesus called it the peace that passes all understanding, because it does not make sense to our simple minds how someone can rest when troubles are raging around them. Yet we know it is not of this world but a heavenly peace from God which is not shaken by external things. The circumstances surrounding Habakkuk appeared so bleak but still he expressed joy and peace.

> Yet I will rejoice in the Lord. I will be joyful in God my saviour. (Habakkuk 3:18)

That is very true for all of us. When God takes our troubles and uses them to build our character, we too can, "to rejoice in the Lord." When we have peace within, it will flow as joy. Our circumstances could still be the same, but we are not the same in our inner being for we are a people who live for a higher purpose.

Gentleness—Jesus described Himself as gentle (Matthew 11:29). When we are in trouble and weary, we can become edgy and restless and this leads to tension and anxiety. It is very unlikely that we will reflect Christ to others in that state. That is why Jesus calls us to go to Him when we are weary and learn from Him. Thus, as we learn of Him then a character of gentleness is the result which Paul said should be evident to all (Philippians 4:5).

Patience—This patience is not like the one that is produced in queues while waiting to be served. This is the kind of patience produced by the Holy Spirit that causes us to waits expectantly in hope for God's promises. It is a patience that demonstrates trust in God when nothing else makes sense, even when we can't understand during the tough times.

Self Control—It might be helpful here to share a personal example of the characteristic of self-control. I got into a financial problem and took a loan—but little did I know I would get into worse trouble. However, God did get me out of it and also gave me wisdom on managing money. I learnt how to refrain from indulgence and impulse buying. I grew in my understanding of good stewardship over the resources given to me by the One who is the source of everything. The Spirit of God awakened me to the truth that I possessed His fruit of self-control even though it was not operating in my life. Through that awakening, I learnt how I should have trusted and waited upon Him instead of settling for quick fixes. I would have saved myself the anxiety caused by the debts and only deal with my financial hardship. I do not want to minimise or simplify the daunting effects of financial hardships but for me self-control was produced out of the mess. Whatever the situation, God uses every opportunity to build our character.

Perseverance—Job's wife looked at him and felt his perseverance was beyond the norm. She did not understand why he kept holding on. She reasoned that the troubles would still kill him, so she advised him to curse God instead of persevering. She did not foresee a good outcome for Job, but through perseverance, he developed godly character. He would have lost that which was more valuable in exchange for the quick fix his wife was offering him. If we desire to experience God's transforming power and His innumerable blessings, then it is crucial to persevere. As we persevere God enables us to keep moving towards the direction of His divine compass even when we cannot see any results or outcome in our suffering.

To Bring Maturity

Every time that as God's children we go through tough times, we are changed in one way or another until we become mature Christians. Sometimes it seems a slow process, but we are meant to grow. Remember we are meant to move from milk to solids and during troubles this progress should happen if we keep our eyes on Him. As we grow, we complain and whine less, for we refuse to be defined by our troubles. Instead we trust in God more and we meditate on His word more. Throughout the process even though we may not see it, we are being built on the unshakable foundation of His eternal love. Maturity enables us to become a people who flow in thankfulness, praise, joy and peace.

Maturity brings a stability that comes from our confidence in knowing that God is ultimately in control. It also brings about a readiness for us to take stock of where our security lies. Do we trust in ourselves, job, money, health, our loved ones, possessions or anything else that we hold dearly? The waves and billows of life can become our stepping stones to a higher level, a place of stability in Christ where we can be instrumental in advancing His kingdom.

To Test and Approve

At the beginning of this chapter I quoted the scripture in Romans which states that God works good even out of what was meant to destroy us. He may see trouble coming and does not stop it, even though He has power to stop it. At other times He stops troubles happening for He is our protector and our shield. If we were to count the number of times that He averts trouble, we would be amazed to discover the vast extent of His love and care for us. The times when He allows trouble is not an indication that He has lost control and that He does not love or care for us. On the contrary, it is for a purpose and for our good.

Therefore, as we explore how God uses our troubles as a test; it is very important that we understand without a shadow of doubt that God has never and will never send any hardship as a punishment. He is not the author of evil and suffering. God is love, and love does not delight in evil, His love protects. He does not punish anyone because Jesus was punished on our behalf. If we say when we are afflicted it is God who is punishing us, then that would imply Jesus did not finish His work—yet we know He said, "It is finished." Remember the scripture in Isaiah chapter 53 clearly says, "He was punished for our transgressions." If we are punished as some of us have thought, then it would imply that we have the capacity to save ourselves. But we are saved grace and grace alone.

Therefore, whenever we are in any trouble we should always remember it is due to the thorns and thistles—the works of the enemy. God walks with us in the valley and He takes over our troubles and uses them as a test for our good. How paramount it is as children of God to ask the Holy Spirit for the gift of discernment to enable us to withstand the temptation of the enemy to accuse God of evil.

There are some moments when we experience a feeling of silence from God. We think we have been abandoned, like He has distanced Himself, and is not listening. But He lives in us and so we are never abandoned. Job had a similar experience when his suffering was beyond what he could bear, and in agony he expressed:

> If only I knew where to find him…. But if I go to the east, he is not
> there; if I go to the west, I do not find him…. When he has tested
> me I will come forth as gold. (Job 23: 3 ;8; 10b)

Job discerned in his heart that God was not punishing him but had taken all his troubles and was now a tool in God's hand being moulded to become, as pure as gold. This was a good outcome for Job and would be so for any Christian. Let us take an ordinary example of students sitting for an exam. During that time there is usually total silence—if someone dropped a pin it would be audible. In that silence, the only probable sound that would be heard is of the students turning the pages of their examination papers. The invigilator or the examiner sits at one side of the room or paces up and down across the room silently. He stays alert for what is going on and keeps checking on any student who might need his help. He also keeps his eyes on the clock to ensure the specified time for the test to end is adhered to. Let us always remember that whenever we are going through tough times where we feel like God has abandoned us, and the suffering is unbearable, that our caring Father stays with us during the test, working gold into our lives, even though we cannot see or feel Him.

The best thing to do is to tell your soul, "Hush!" and then concentrate on turning the pages of your Bible to the familiar passages of God's promises and let them become your pillar of support. Remember also to say, "when He has tested me; I will come forth as gold." We say it not for the sake of positive thinking but as an indication that we are aligning with God's will. God delights in such an attitude, and it will make the process more bearable for us. Then we will not be drawn from the potter's hands by well-meaning friends like Job's wife.

If we allow friends, family or our church leaders to draw us from the potter's hands then we miss the opportunity to be moulded to become like Christ. God's shaping in our lives will then be incomplete and must be continued through the next trial that will come our way. However, if we identify the test and rest as we allow God to have His way, then nothing is wasted. As we spend time meditating on those familiar promises from the word, the Holy Spirit gives us strength, hope, a reason to continue as we move from milk to solids.

To Transform Our Prayer Life

> Pray continually, give thanks in all circumstances, for this is God's will for you in Christ. (1 Thessalonians 5:17)

There are many reasons why people pray, and we discussed a few of the reasons earlier. The greatest reason for prayer is that God's children may build an intimate relationship with God. During troubled times, our prayers can take on two dimensions. Sometimes it can be very dry and just plodding as pain and agony sap our strength to pray. At other times, prayer can bring heaven on earth by our desperation for a breakthrough. We can eliminate the two-dimensional pattern of prayers in order to follow Jesus' example. As we do that then the outcome would be a transformed prayer life of intimacy that our Father longs for.

Though the weariness and lethargy of our troubles steal our desire to pray, it is important to remind ourselves that the Holy Spirit helps us in our weakness. As we let Him take over, He prompts us to pray rather than to plod or give up. God takes the prayers of His children seriously, therefore we will make every effort to pray as we are led, knowing our prayers are not in vain.

But the prayer of the upright pleases him. (Proverbs 15:8b)

He hears the prayer of the righteous. (Proverbs 15:29b)

Understanding the importance of prayer and the reasons why we pray will increase our desire to pray, and as a result our relationship with God will move to new heights of intimacy. Prayer is a way of life for a believer, a channel to keep us in touch with our Father in heaven, not merely a call for help when we are in trouble. As we spend quality time of prayer in communion with Him, we are assured that His ears are attentive to us regardless of location, time, or pattern. We can simply talk with Him because He loves us and delights in the prayers of His children. However even when we fail to keep in touch with Him, He understands and knows us and meets us where we are in our time of need. He does not check when we last prayed or for what reason. His love does not keep a record of wrongs. All He desires is that we keep in communion with Him.

All through Jesus' life here on earth, prayer was a very important aspect of His relationship with His Father. From His example, there is much we can learn, which can transform our prayer lives.

a) He maintained a constant communication with His Father (Mark 1:35)
b) He spent unhurried time with Him (Mark 1:35).
c) He understood His Father's business and therefore found time to connect with Him in prayer making sure He never lost touch with what His Father was doing.
d) He understood that prayers are not only to be said when in trouble thus He prayed continually in any season.
e) He prayed unconcerned about being heard by others but by His Father.
f) He prayed at any time and at any place even in His busy schedule as He walked, taught and performed miracles.

When Jesus went to the mountain to pray as recorded in Mark 1:35, He did not attract any attention. It was early when many would be cuddled in the comfort of their beds. He did not go there because He was in trouble. He might not have prayed many words (though we are not told). But when He taught his disciples how to pray, He emphasized that praying with many words is not what makes us heard by our Father in heaven. Therefore, prayer is much more than we imagine or make of it.

When I was growing up, I had daily conversations with my father, and this helps me to understand what prayer is. I did not have to write it down on a piece of paper or in a note book and it was not the same conversation all the time. It was open and based on the relationship we had as a father and child. These were such precious and priceless moments to sit and chat and share what was in my heart and there were many things to converse about. They were very special moments, times of exploring, learning, asking, listening and never one sided and not only when we sat together.

I did not approach him only when I needed him to do something or with a long list of things that I needed. How would you feel as a parent if your children talked to you only when they wanted something? It would send a message to those around you of a broken relationship. It would also be a lonely experience for the father who is communicated with only when there is trouble or need. I know our Father in heaven is God and perfect and cannot be compared to the fathers of this world; yet He came to our level through Jesus and delights to spend time with us.

We are His children, loved and not restricted on how we should relate to Him. He invites us to approach His throne boldly with confidence and assurance. We can sit at His feet or walk along the way and commune with Him in our hearts. During the times that we commune with Him, an intimacy develops and grows to greater heights and depths in Him. Jesus spent a lot of time with His Father in prayer and during those moments He was changing the world because He knew the Father's heart and business. We too will change the situations in our lives, on behalf of others, and in the world through spending time in prayer.

As we desire to see His Name hallowed, His Kingdom come, His will done in all the earth as it is in heaven, our prayers must be different. We will pray with reverence, recognition of the One who is able to change the world through our prayers by the power of the Holy Spirit. Jesus warns us in the scripture not to pray like the pagans or the hypocrites (Matthew 6:5–8). Religious prayers were based on mechanical, ritual pattern and not on a reverent awe of God. If we pray with reverence, we have no doubt that He hears us and such prayers are powerful and effectual. As we pray, we will not be in a rush, it will not be just a plodding but transformation will be the end result. Our transformed prayer life then remains our way of living regardless of our circumstances.

The afflictions that were meant to destroy us instead bring about the good outcome of a transformed prayer life. We will be a people who delight to pray, not only when troubles come but who humbly present their requests with thanksgiving to God. We will see God's Kingdom come in the earth as it is in heaven through prayer. Therefore, as we form the habit of praying continually, the venue, time, and posture, are secondary. What matters and is of concern to God is a heart of reverence.

To Equip and Prepare Us for Ministry

> The Father of compassion and the God of all comfort, who comforts us in all our troubles, so that we can comfort those in any trouble with the comfort we ourselves have received from God (2 Corinthians 1:3–4).

God allows us to go through painful experiences as a way of equipping us for ministry to others. All over the world people are in turmoil and desperate situations. They have no answers, without hope and are under the weight of many troubles. They hold on to whatever hope this world offers, but it disappoints them. As we are brought through the tough times in our lives, God opens our eyes to see, and softens our hearts to feel, the needs of others. He equips us with everything we need for others. He shapes and changes us in the heat of affliction to be fit for His purpose. Sometimes when people are grieving, we say words unthinkingly which add more pain than comfort. After we have gone through the pain of loss, one good outcome is that from henceforth we choose our words wisely—words that bring healing, comfort and hope to others in their grief of loss.

The comfort which we have received from God is what we give to those in trouble. Equipped people will hear of those involved in national disasters and not remark that they are being punished by God. Instead they will understand that creation groans desiring to be delivered from its fallen state. The Bible says God is always thinking good thoughts towards us. After being prepared and equipped by Him, we too will have good thoughts and an attitude of concern towards others in whatever circumstances they are in.

Just like doctors or lawyers, who must go through years of training before they practice, so it is for those that Jesus has enrolled in His school of life. From the day we give our lives to the Lord until our final breath, the training, equipping and preparation continues. However, during afflictions the process is intensified as God takes the troubles which the enemy meant for evil and turns them into tools for equipping us, making us fit for His purpose. As we are healed and restored, God will use our changed lives to do the same for others in the world through us.

To Let Us Enter into God's Rest

To enter into God's rest is very important. Rest is not only a good outcome when we are afflicted but essential in our walk with God. Despite the many miracles God performed for the Israelites they never entered His rest. However, God remained faithful and was there with them throughout their journey bringing a good outcome for every trouble.

> The Lord replied, "my presence will go with you, and I will give you rest. (Exodus 33:14)

His presence goes with us too and we are to rest. We read in Hebrews chapters 3 and 4 that we must enter His rest—and although it speaks of a future rest, there is an emphasis on the here and now. Many of our troubles linger due to our own lack of entering God's rest. Every trouble must leave us in a better state than the previous one and the secret to this is walking in the knowledge of God's presence with us and

His promised rest. When we are secure because of His presence with us, then we can rest, for He is the giver of rest.

The Bible tells us that while Joseph was in prison, he maintained a joyful countenance as he continued with his daily life of serving God and others around him. This is because he had understood the secret of entering God's rest and radiated a visible joy and peace to his fellow prisoners. Joseph had every reason to despair considering he had committed no crime to warrant imprisonment. Reading his story, we note that there were times he felt sorrowful, and moments of frustration and loneliness due to separation from his family. However, even in trouble he served God faithfully and became a blessing to others who were in prison with him.

To Manifest His Glory

Finally, we said God always brings an end to our suffering, and just like He did to others He will do for us too.

> The Lord blessed the latter part of Job's life more than the first. ...
> After this, Job lived a hundred and forty years, he saw his children
> and their children to the fourth generation. And so he died old and
> full of years (Job 42:12, 16–17)

Job did not suffer forever. Similarly, Joseph did not stay in the pit, or prison for ever, he was reconciled to his family. He then allocated them a place to settle and also saved many nations. He was put in charge of the whole land of Egypt (Genesis 41:41). Through his gift of interpreting dreams, God turned all that the enemy meant for evil into a good outcome.

As I bring this chapter to a close let me emphasise the truths we have explored. It would be a sad outcome for any child of God, to go through pain and suffering and remain the same. Therefore, we must embrace our trials as a catalyst for change in our character, prayer life, our love for God and others. Adversity must lead us to a level of a deeper intimacy with God. May God help us to be equally teachable and patient during times of troubles that we too like Joseph and Job will receive a good outcome as we fulfil His purpose.

God has the final word, not the difficulties in our lives. We come out intact, and our lives become richer, fuller and effective in His kingdom. Then our cry deep down in our hearts would be the same cry Jesus made, "Father be glorified!"

However, a child of God must always be ready, in suffering or in good times, for the final outcome of good, which means going home to where we belong

Prayer

Father we thank You for Your word which assures us that all things work together for our good because Jesus made this possible. Give us teachable and obedient hearts by the power of Your Holy Spirit to enter the rest that we have found in You. Amen.

CHAPTER 6: LOOKING BEYOND

I consider that our present sufferings are not worth comparing with the glory that will be revealed in us. (Romans 8:18)

In scripture, a Christian is described as a sojourner, a runner, and an ambassador. All these titles have a similar connotation—that we are on the move. These titles also suggest that we do not belong in this present world. There is a glory waiting to be revealed in us that surpasses any suffering. We are only here to do our Father's business in His world; we are not settlers.

As it is you do not belong to the world, but I have chosen you out of the world. (John 15:19)

Instead they were longing for a better country--a heavenly one. Therefore God is not ashamed to be called their God, for he has prepared a city for them. (Hebrews 11:16)

In light of this, it is clear that if we do not look beyond this world then we are in danger of settling. Either our comforts or our troubles can keep us focused in the here and now. Once we allow this to happen even the good outcomes in our lives are only beneficial for a while and there is no long-term gain or progress.

Let us take the example of the hurdles race in the Olympic Games and compare this with the race of going to heaven. Every competitor jumps hurdle by hurdle and continues with the race to the finish line. The hurdles are usually arranged in the middle of the course, not at the beginning or at the end.

My observation is that even when the runner knocks down a hurdle, he does not stop to pick it up as the focus is on the finish line. The runner keeps moving on and is never concerned of any distraction even where there may be injury. Finishing and keeping the mind focused on the finish matters more to the runner than injury. When we give our lives to the Lord, our race to heaven begins, and that is the reason why the Christian is described as a runner. On the journey between now and the finish line troubles can come upon us, like those hurdles, and we must keep jumping and pressing on. We need to trust wholeheartedly and to remember that we are not alone—Jesus remains with us all the way, cheering us to keep going.

As we keep our eyes upon Jesus the author and finisher of our faith, He enables us to look beyond the suffering of this world to the glory that will be ours at the end of the race. If Jesus is the One who will make us perfect and finish His work in us as God's children, then we need to keep jumping every hurdle. As we see Him who endured the cross, we too will have the courage and ability to look beyond this life. We cannot quit being children of God. We have been adopted into His family and we are on the journey to join Him. According to the above scripture, we are going is a place that is already prepared, and which is permanent, but we must keep running until we get there. The ability to look beyond is based on three essential elements—identity, purpose and destiny.

Identity: We Know Who We Are

Without an identity in Jesus Christ we do not know who we are and therefore we cannot look beyond our troubles. Knowing our identity in Christ is the most powerful thing in the life of a child of God. It drives us forward in purpose so that we are not threatened by our circumstances. We become a people who are resilient to whatever comes our way because Christ is the centre of our lives. As He gives our lives meaning and purpose then we have a reason to keep moving, a desire and drive to look beyond the afflictions of this life.

A life without purpose will keep us in a state of just getting along and doing what everybody else is doing so long as it seems good. With such a concept we view our troubles through the world's lens which ultimately leads to despair with nothing beyond. If Christ is not the centre of our lives, we have no hope beyond this world and therefore no real identity. It is our identity in Him that keeps us in motion as the runner who will not be derailed by what happens along the way.

For in him we live and move and have our being. (Acts 17:28)

We are not a people who just happened to appear out of nowhere and came to be; we are the "offspring of God," as we read further along in Acts chapter 17. We are not put in this world by mistake, we were predestined by the Almighty God himself and it is in Him our identity is found. We have the very DNA of God as overcomers and finishers, therefore we look beyond our present troubles because we are propelled forward by the very life of God that is within us. The scripture above draws the three essential elements for looking beyond. To have our being in Jesus, that is *identity*. To live in Him is to have find *purpose*, and if it is in Him we move then this means we have a *destiny*.

Purpose: We Know What We Are Here For

> In fact, for this reason I was born. And for this I came into the world to testify to the truth. (John 18:37b)

Jesus experienced troubles that no one else in all creation can ever go through. He took on Himself all the troubles of the whole world. Though He had taken such a heavy weight upon Himself, it did not cloud the understanding of His purpose. We are those who are called as ambassadors of heaven and imitators of Christ, asserting without a shadow of doubt that we know why we are here in this world. We are ambassadors representing a country called heaven. Without such knowledge trouble will put us off balance and cloud our understanding of what is significant. The life which Jesus has given us keeps us looking beyond to the eternally significant.

Jesus finished everything that His Father had sent Him to do. He has made us heirs with Him and has given us the privilege of putting our mark on that finished work. With confidence we must declare that "this is the purpose for which we were born." Sometimes the danger of giving up can become great, but as we keep our eyes on Jesus who is in us and is greater than our problems, then we continue looking beyond. At the climax of the darkest moment ever to be experienced or known, Jesus cried out, "It is finished!" In the greatest agony Jesus knew who He was, His purpose and where He was going. He looked beyond the present and He now calls us to do the same. There are others too, who have gone before us and have completed the race who took the same view; the faithful followers of God.

> They were stoned, they were sawn in two, were tempted, were slain with the sword. They wandered about in sheepskins and goatskins being destitute, afflicted tormented. (Hebrews 11:37) (NKJV)

They encountered every trouble that is imaginable. Yet despite everything they continued the race that was marked before them because they were looking beyond their afflictions. They looked towards the finish line and we know that they are part of the big cloud of witnesses cheering us on to keep moving and to looking beyond.

Sometimes we feel like giving up, due to the many challenges we face every day, but we have to keep reminding ourselves that in Christ we are more than conquerors. God has called us to fulfil His purpose in the reverent knowledge of who He is and not fear anything—especially not the troubles that come our way. The enemy and the voice of reason may want us to fear and tremble because of our afflictions but let us keep looking beyond them no matter what. Like the runner let us jump every hurdle and encourage one another along the journey.

Our Destiny: We Know Where We Are Going

A few years ago, I went to Leicester on an errand. I left Manchester in the morning and was expected back in the evening. As it was June, I dressed very casually, but by the time I completed my errand in the evening it had turned very chilly. Suddenly I felt very cold and wished I was indoors; but I still had a fifteen-minute walk to the train station before I could find cover.

When I got to the train station, I was informed that the train was delayed by two hours. All I could think of was how I now had double trouble. I would have succumbed to going back to look for an alternative, but I opted to be patient and persevere. Throughout my waiting, I could not help listening to every tick of my wrist watch, which sounded like it was ticking slower than usual. I knew it was my imagination—the ticking was just as it has always been, but my ears heard something different. Even in times of adversity whilst we are waiting for a breakthrough, we must not go by what we see or hear of our situation. Our imaginations can make us believe something untrue, like I did with the ticking of my watch. That is why as Christians we must no longer live according to our senses but by faith alone.

However, my waiting was not in vain for after the time specified, the train did finally come, and I was so sure it was taking me to Manchester where I was meant to be. My family were still up and waiting for me, ready with a warm welcome and a hot cup of tea. As I sipped my steaming cup of tea, I forgot the cold and the wait at the station, which was now history.

This example may sound nothing compared with the pain and suffering we go through in our lives, but my point is that we are here for a purpose. When that work is done, we will have no need of staying here. We must not lose sight of this, for as we persevere in moving forward and looking beyond, we will make progress even if we do not see it. With the knowledge that Jesus is our guide, the light on our path, and the One who knows the way, then our arrival is sure. When Paul was going through the most severe difficulties he remained in his identity, his purpose and his destiny. The Bible says:

> Sorrowful, yet always rejoicing; poor yet making many rich; having nothing, and yet possessing everything. (2 Corinthians 6:10)

How could Paul possibly be sorrowful and yet rejoicing, poor and making others rich? The answer is simple, because it is based on an eternal perspective. The knowledge of his identity made him serve in making others rich. He sounds like one who had already received a good outcome of his troubles, yet he was still in trouble. His circumstances had not changed but he was now living in a state of unshakable character which had developed through times of hardship. We do not rejoice because of the troubles but in the Lord and as we serve Him, we make many rich with riches that are of eternal value. It is through His sufficient grace, courage and strength that we accomplish the work He has given us. As we continue with the work with a winner's attitude, we emerge intact with a clearer perspective on trusting God until we finish the race.

The faithful ones in Hebrews 11 kept looking beyond their circumstances to the city God was preparing for them. That is the same place that we long for—the heavenly home—and we are all invited to dwell there forever. There is a day that is coming when we will join them and the One who created, loved and rescued us and has a glorious future for us. If only we can grasp with our eyes of faith, that glorious future even when every part of us is screaming due to our afflictions then we can look beyond our troubles to a brighter destiny.

Therefore, it is my hope that as Christians you know who you are, why you exist and where you are headed, for if you do then you can look beyond any trouble. Every ambassador eventually returns to his country, the sojourner finally reaches his destination and the runner reaches the finishing line. That means we will have no need to stay here when our work is done for our destination is heaven.

Prayer

We thank You our Father that You enable us through Jesus Christ to look beyond our difficult times. Grant us strength, grace and hope daily by the power of the Holy Spirit to continue till we reach the finish line. Amen.

CHAPTER 7: SALVATION FOR ALL

Just as trouble comes to us all, hope is also given to us all through salvation in Jesus Christ. Our hope that there is an end to our sufferings comes from having a personal relationship with Jesus. He is the One who came to save us and rescue us from all our troubles. Without salvation then we have no hope for this life and we cannot have a good outcome from our trials.

On this side of eternity, we are so privileged to have a God who is always doing good to all He has made. He leads us towards repentance, through His kindness, long suffering and patience. His desire is that no one should perish. On the other side of eternity however, there will be such great trouble for those who have not accepted the gift of salvation. Instead of the privilege of God's goodness there will be separation from God forever. God's goodness cannot be measured, and it is for all mankind—those who love Him and even those who do not.

> He causes the sun to rise on the evil and good and sends rain on the righteous and the unrighteous. (Matthew 5:45)

He does this for everyone He has made, because of His love and mercy that through His kind deeds towards each one of us we may be led to know Him. His sun has risen upon us all today, giving us a chance to come out of darkness into His light. His desire is that we escape the trouble of separation from God which is inevitable on the other side of eternity. This will be separation without hope for ever.

I am writing this chapter to you personally if you are not in Christ Jesus. This is solely for you as a reminder of how God loves you and that without responding to His love you are lost. Salvation is the best gift, given to us only through Jesus, for only He can save us from the trouble that is to come. In the chapter on the good outcome we discussed how God turns our troubles into good. Sad to say, eternal separation from God can never be compared to the troubles of this life. Eternal trouble will never have any good outcome. For as happened in the case of the five foolish virgins—once the door was shut, it was never opened again—so it will be for those who have refused the truth now. Once the door of God's grace is shut, it will never be reopened (Matthew 25:1–12).

The God who loves us so much and came to rescue us will one day close the door and bring this day of grace to an end. The sun and rain He gives us all on this side of eternity will cease. I do not wish to frighten anyone who does not have a relationship with Jesus. It is all about love and because God loves you, there is no need to fear. There is good news for you; there is hope today. Take the chance; do not let it pass you by. Do not wait any longer, today is the day of salvation—the best of all outcomes.

This is called good news and it is not a coincidence that you have picked this book. If you do not yet know Jesus as your Lord and Saviour, it is not too late to make the best decision of your whole lifetime. The sunshine and rain are the signs of blessing that God pours out every day for us all to enjoy. But there is much more to enjoy when He lives in you as your Lord and Saviour, joy that will last beyond this life because He loves you.

His mercy and grace overflow every day. His arms are still outstretched to embrace you, but He cannot make that decision for you. If today I bought a gift for someone and stretched out my hands to give it to the person, they can take it or leave it. The gift of salvation has also been made available to us all, but the choice of receiving it is left to each one of us. It is too costly that no amount of money can buy and yet both the rich and the poor can afford it. We can receive it by faith. Although it is freely given, it cost Jesus His life, the highest cost imaginable.

A caution for you; do not let the devil deceive you that you can have eternal life through your own efforts or good works, observing the law, or fulfilling the requirements of Holy Communion, baptism and confirmation. These may follow later. The thief on the cross never had a chance for all that, but accepting Jesus as his Lord and saviour gave him a guarantee of eternal life. Salvation cost Jesus His life therefore nothing else can be added, His sacrifice was complete.

A second lie the devil might tell you is that since God is love, full of mercy, compassionate, just and fair we do not need to be saved to have eternal life. It is tempting to believe that, but it is not what God says in His word.

He is patient with you, not wanting anyone to perish, but everyone to come to repentance. (2 Peter3:9b)

83

The following are simple steps that you can take to receive the free gift of eternal life:

a) Acknowledge that you have sinned and fallen short of God's standards. We fall short of His standards when we live in our own way and become the masters of our own life.

We all like sheep have gone astray each of us has turned on his own way; and the Lord has laid on Him (Jesus) the iniquity of us all. (Isaiah 53:6)

b) Accept Jesus by faith. He washes us clean with His blood from our iniquities and we relinquish ownership of our life and give Him permission to be Lord. His love is so gentle and therefore He never pushes His way or puts pressure on us.

For it is with your heart that you believe and are justified, and it is with your mouth that you confess and are saved. (Romans 10:10)

c) Our name is then written in the book of life to complete the adoption process that we are God's children.

d) Then God fills us with His Holy Spirit. He is our guarantee and teaches us how to build our relationship with Him through prayer, studying His word and fellowshipping with Him and His family (other Christians). By walking with Jesus, in time you will start to understand what adversity is about, though not fully on this side of eternity. However, you become eternally secure no matter what life throws at you.

Here we come to the close of this subject of afflictions and of how the whole creation was subjected to suffering due to the fall. Thankfully the fall is not where the story ends otherwise there would be no hope for any of us. Jesus took not only our sins but suffering and death as well. He left nothing undone, everything was put under Him. Everything bows to Him, even any adversity. He is above all things in the whole of the universe.

> In putting everything under Him, God left nothing that is not subject to Him. Yet at present we do not see everything subject to Him. But we see Jesus who was made a little lower than the angels, now crowned with glory and honour because He suffered death, so that by the grace of God He might taste death for everyone. (Hebrews 2:8–9)

He is in control; everything else is subject to change but He remains. (Psalm 102:25–28). He is the Alpha and Omega and to Him be glory forever. Amen.

EPILOGUE: FINISHING WELL

I started this book in the year 2013. Before that I was struck by a tormenting and agonising skin disease. I was in anguish and in desperation. Things did not get any better because of the many times I prayed, the many scriptures I quoted and claimed, or the many repeated prescriptions from the doctor. I rebuked the devil many times. I did everything that I could possibly do, even confessing any known sins. I trusted in God, I had faith, I attended many conferences and was prayed for, but my suffering did not ease or improve.

A year passed, and another, and more years; surely, I was not looking for a quick remedy for it had lingered over quite some years and it was getting worse every day. I gave myself credit that I was not asking for a quick fix, but that healing was overdue. I had persevered and waited for long enough. That was my opinion which was based on the pain I was experiencing but God knows all things, in control and with perfect timing.

Sometimes I experienced bouts of depression and despair, but only for a while and the Lord would lift me up and I would know that I must keep moving as I was not alone. His grace has been sufficient every day and throughout the many years that I have been afflicted. His presence has been undeniable, though not so obvious to me as my focus most of the times has been on my health. All throughout this journey however, I have kept holding on to His promises as my pillar of support and refusing to believe otherwise.

It is a mystery why some never get healed or get answers to some difficult situations even though they have prayed and believed. The final analysis is that God is sovereign, His love remains, and He does not delight in our suffering. As for us, we only know in part (1 Corinthians 13:12).

As you close this book you may be going through troubles that you feel are more than you can bear, and wonder whether it will ever end. Finishing well is crucial and it is what matters—not the rewards, though they are always included in the package. I have now recovered fully, but I can say it has been the most traumatic and challenging experience of my life. Every day in my agony I had to keep reminding myself to live in hope, to trust in God's promises, to know I am secure in His everlasting arms and to serve Him without wavering. Today like Job and Joseph and many others wherever they are in the whole world, I can declare with confidence and without a shadow of doubt, "Jesus never fails and is never late!"

May this too be your proclamation that you will live in hope, trusting in God's promises and knowing how secure you are in His everlasting arms. He loves you and will make a way where it seems impossible. Remember that giving up is not your portion. What the enemy meant for evil will not destroy you. The tenacity to keep on going will lead you to finish well. As for me I will be praying for you that your faith will not fail. In Jesus name, Amen.